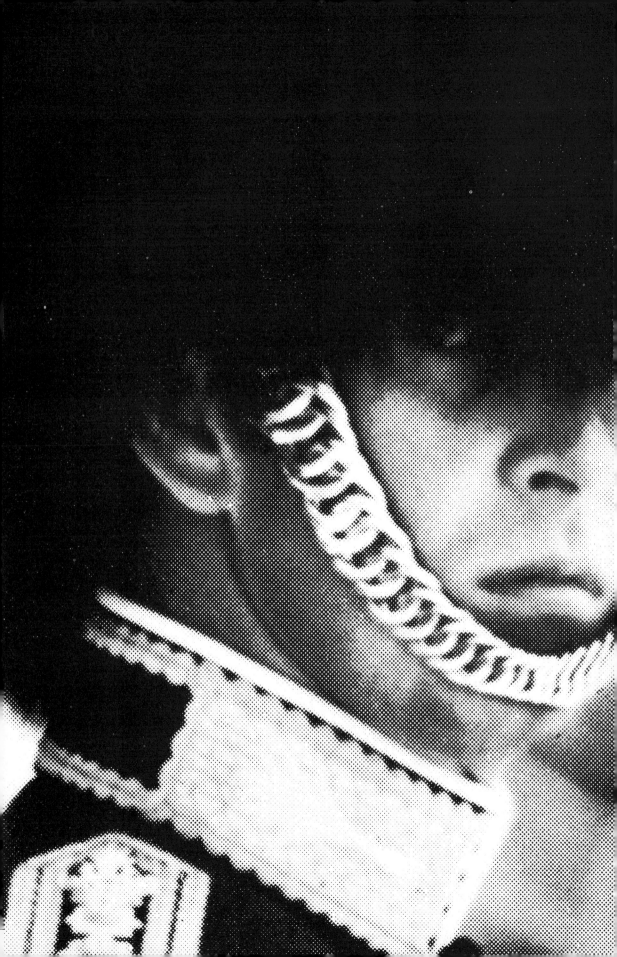

Charles In His Own Words.

Compiled by Rosemary York.
Designed by Perry Neville.

Exclusive distributors:
Book Sales Limited,
78 Newman Street, London W1P 3LA.
Quick Fox,
Angus & Robertson, Publishers,
Sydney, Australia.

Omnibus Press
London/New York/Sydney/Cologne.

Published 1981 by Omnibus Press
(a division of Book Sales Limited).

Book concept, design & origination:
Perry Neville.
Design assistant: Gill Lockhart.
Picture research: Susan Ready.
Original series styling: Pearce Marchbank.
Cover photograph: Camera Press/Les Wilson.

This book © copyright 1981 Omnibus Press.
Introduction © copyright 1981 Rosemary York.

ISBN 0-86001-861-X.
UK Order No. OP 41151.

Typeset by G.W.Young Photosetters Limited,
Brighton Road, Surbiton, Surrey.
Printed in England by William Clowes
(Beccles) Limited, Beccles and London.

Prince Charles is a favourite of the Press and has been the subject of many "official" biographies.

He has only to fall from a horse or remark on a pretty girl to make the front page – not just in Britain, but throughout the world.

From the announcement of his birth to his choice of a fairytale princess, his whole life has been recorded and photographed without mercy. Yet, he talks very little about himself and rarely gives interviews.

Here his comments, thoughts and humour on almost every subject have been selected from the archives of newspapers, radio and television and collected together for the first time. He talks about school, his family and the problems of making friends, his hobbies, sports and, of course, his marriage.

Charles In His Own Words presents a composite picture of the private individual behind the public myth. He emerges as a Twentieth Century prince with a modest, witty and perceptive view of the world. *Rosemary York.*

WITH PRINCESS ANNE/PHOTO CECIL BEATON

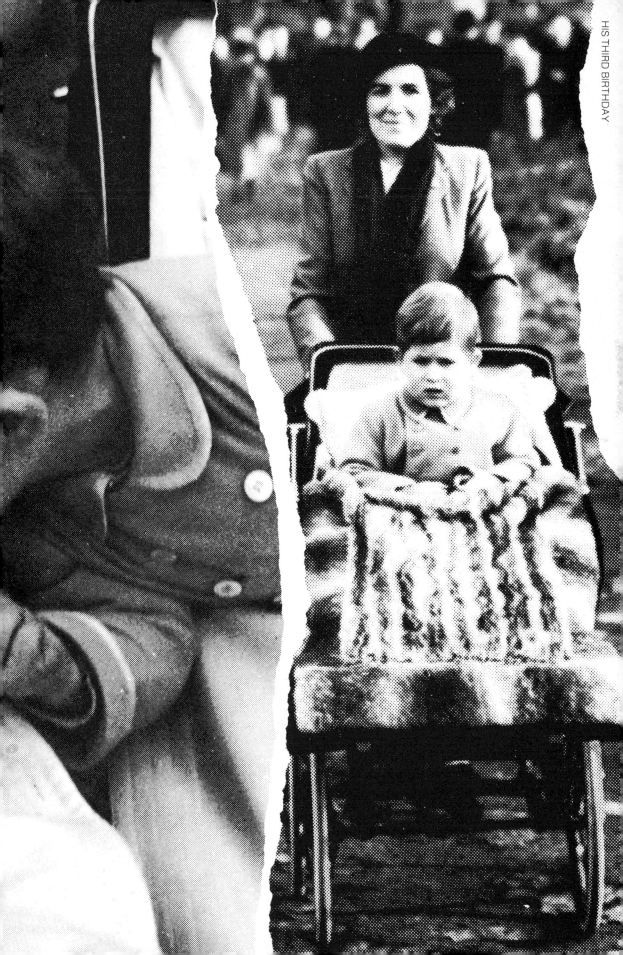

Schooldays.

Mummy, what *are* schoolboys? (Age 8)

Charles went first to Hill House, then Cheam, and eventually to Gordonstoun:

I suppose I could have gone to the local comprehensive or the local grammar, but I'm not sure it would have done me much good. I think a public school gives you a great deal of self-discipline and experience and responsibility, and it is the responsibility which is so worthwhile.

It's very rewarding and it gives you the added confidence in yourself that you have the ability to do something for other people, and they trust you to do it. I think this is very important.

You learn the way they say the monkey learns: watching its parents! On the whole, you pick it up as you go along.

I did some constitutional history when I was at school, but I didn't get very far with it. You can't teach children a great deal of such a complicated and sophisticated subject by making them read books or write essays. After school, I had to do so many other things that there wasn't time or need to get down to it as I would have liked.

That's the advantage of meeting a number of people who know a lot about it, and talking to them. The Lord Chancellor, for instance. Now I'm going to have more time in this country, I'm going to try to learn more about it.

I wasn't made to follow in my father's footsteps in any sense or in any way. His attitude was very simple: he told me what were the pros and cons of all the possibilities and what he thought was best. Then he left me to decide.

I freely subjected myself to what he thought best because I saw how wise he

AT CHEAM SCHOOL/ PHOTO KEYSTONE

was. By the time I had to be educated, I had perfect confidence in my father's judgement.

When children are young, of course, you have to decide for them. I'm talking about the later stage when they are old enough to share in decisions about themselves.

Gordonstoun.

I'm glad I went to Gordonstoun. It wasn't the toughness of the place – that's all much exaggerated by reports – it was the general character of the education there. Kurt Hahn's principles provide an education which tries to balance the physical and mental, with an emphasis on self-reliance to develop a rounded human being.

I didn't enjoy school as much as I might have, but that was only because I'm happier at home than anywhere else.

Gordonstoun developed my will-power and self-control. It helped me to discipline myself, and I think that discipline, not in the sense of making you bath in cold water, but in the Latin sense – giving shape and form and tidiness to your

life – is the most important thing your education can do.

Dr. Kurt Hahn, the founder, did not exactly require boys to undergo initiation ceremonies, but believed that a boy must challenge himself and discover his own level of endurance and will-power. He believed in the acquisition of self-knowledge and self-discipline.

My experience was that this worked surprisingly well and that's why I'm so keen that others should experience it.

I'm always astonished by the amount of rot that is talked about Gordonstoun and the careless use of ancient clichés to describe it. It was only tough in that it demanded more from you as an individual, mentally and physically, than most other schools.

I believe it taught me a great deal about myself and my own abilities and disabilities, and it taught me to take challenges and initiatives.

At my school we went in for "adventure." We ran our own fire brigade, we had our own sea rescue service, mountain rescue, surf life-saving, coastguard, etc. It *was* adventure. And we were damn good. We used to say that the reason why the local fire brigade sometimes didn't call us out was because we were better than they were.

On the problems of making friends at school:

At Gordonstoun, you could hear them accusing other people of sucking-up and this is a problem. But it's one of those things that you learn through experience – how to sense who are the ones who are sucking-up, and who are being genuine.

Of course the trouble is, that very often, the worst people come first and the really nice people hang back because they don't want to be accused of sucking-up.

On a school trip round the Hebrides, fourteen-year-old Charles drank an illegal glass of brandy in a hotel bar. The incident made front page news around the world:

Well, I thought it was the end of the earth. I was all ready to pack my bags and leave for Siberia.

We went to Stornoway and I went to a hotel to have a meal. While we were waiting for a table, a lot of people were looking in the windows, so I thought,

ARRIVING AT GORDONSTOUN/PHOTO CENTRAL PRESS

"I can't bear this any more," and went off somewhere else. The only other place was the bar.

Having never been into a bar before, the first thing I thought of doing was having a drink, of course. It seemed the most sensible thing. And being terrified, not knowing what to do, I said the first drink that came into my head, which happened to be cherry brandy, because I'd drunk it before, when it was cold, out shooting.

Hardly had I taken a sip when the whole world exploded around my ears. That's all.

Timbertop.

Charles went to Timbertop School in Australia:

It was a very sad moment, of course, leaving England, seeing one's father and sister standing on the tarmac and waving goodbye. I found the moment I was in the air, it was much better. When I got to Australia, the people were so friendly and so welcoming.

I must admit I'd been apprehensive about going there because I'd heard that the Australians were critical and, perhaps,

would show their feelings. I was worried about how I would appear to them, but after I'd been there an hour I found I'd had absolutely no need to worry.

The school is situated in the foothills of the Dividing Range and all the buildings are extraordinarily well hidden from view as there are gum-trees everywhere. The boys live in units, or bungalow-type buildings, of which there are nine, holding fifteen boys apiece.

The Chapel is in the centre and is in the shape of a continuous steep roof that reaches to the ground. Behind the altar, there is a huge window that looks out on to a series of ridges receding into the distance.

When I arrived here, everything was very dry and brown, but now it is all green since the early rains came.

I've been out to several farms in the area and have watched some shearing being done. I was asked to try my hand, but of course made rather a mess of it, and left a somewhat shredded sheep.

Everyone asks how Australia compares with England, which is a very difficult question, as there isn't really a comparison. The mountains are so different from Scotland because there are no ordered fields, but rolling hills covered in grass, with gum-trees dotted about everywhere.

I came over here expecting boiling weather all the time but one soon discovered one's error, as it can certainly become very cold, especially during winter, while it's summer term at Gordonstoun.

A popular cry seems to be that Timbertop is very similar to Gordonstoun.

From what I make of it, Timbertop is very individual. All the boys are virtually the same age, fourteen to fifteen; there are no prefects, and the masters do all the work that boys otherwise do in a school. This way, I think there is much more contact between masters and boys, as everyone is placed in the same sort of situation.

There is a lot of wood-chopping done here, but I'm afraid it's very essential as

the boys' boilers have to be stoked with logs, and the kitchen uses a huge number. The first week I was here I was made to go out and chop up logs on a hillside in boiling hot weather. I could hardly see my hands for blisters after that!

You had to go on expeditions every weekend into the bush and you had two "cross-countries" a week. The first ones I had when I got there were absolutely horrifying. It was ninety degrees in the shade, with flies everywhere, and you sort of ran around amongst the kangaroos and things. Dust and everything.
   Then one played fairly fierce games. They weren't organised games like football or anything like that: you chopped down trees.

Some boys managed to walk fantastic distances over a weekend of four days or less, covering up to two hundred miles.

The furthest I've been is sixty or seventy miles in three days, climbing about five peaks on the way. At the campsite, the cooking is done on an open fire in a trench. You have to be very careful in hot weather that you don't start a bush fire, and at the beginning of this term there was a total fire-ban in force, so we ate all the tinned food cold.
   Apart from that, you virtually have to inspect every inch of ground ... in case there are ants or other ghastly creatures. There is one species called Bull Ants which are three-quarters of an inch long or more and they bite like mad!

In between all these diversions, work has to fit in somewhere. In fact, the weeks just seem to be a useful means of filling up the gaps between the weekends, which come round very quickly.
   Obviously, work can't be taken quite as seriously as in an ordinary school, but there are classes all morning after Chapel

at 8.45 a.m. and there is a two-hour prep period in the evening.

Each afternoon after classes, which end at three o'clock, there are jobs which are rather equivalent to PW but involve chopping and splitting wood, feeding the pigs, cleaning out fly-traps (revolting glass bowls seething with flies and very ancient meat) or picking up bits of paper round the school.

There is no organised sport in the form of field games, but each Wednesday there is either a tug o' war between the boys' units, or houses, or, if it's hot, there is swimming or perhaps someone is feeling sufficiently cruel to organise a race that involves carrying half a tree for a certain distance.

I almost convinced one or two Australians outside the school that we rustled kangaroos at Timbertop and that we performed this art by creeping up on them from behind, grabbing them by the tail and flicking them over onto their backs, where you had them at your mercy.

More than any other experience, those years opened my eyes. You are judged there on how people see you and feel about you. There are no assumptions there. Having a title and being a member of the upper classes as often as not mitigates against you.

In Australia, you have to fend for yourself. I was fairly shy when I was

younger but Australia certainly cured me of that.

There may be limitations I have to accept, but not mixing isn't one of them. I do mix. It's one of the privileges of my position. If you say, "Well, you haven't lived with men who do this or that, or who haven't got this or that," I say, "Quite so, but I've *met* some of the people who live with them and do know about them – and that's more than many thousands of people in this country have the chance to do."

I absolutely adored it. I couldn't have enjoyed it more. The most wonderful experience I've ever had, I think.

That school's probably the reason why, whenever I come back to Australia, I experience a curious and inexplicable sensation that I belong.

Cambridge.

I'm one of those stupid bums who went to university. Well, I think it's helped me. You see, I really wanted to go to university because I felt that I hadn't had enough education at school, and I felt that going to university for another three years would round it off and give me just that much more.

WITH HIS TUTOR/PHOTO CENTRAL PRESS

It would be marvellous to have three years when you are not bound by anything, not married, and haven't any particular job.

His first day at Trinity:

All I could see from the Mini on arrival were serried ranks of trousered legs, from which I had to distinguish those of the Master and the Senior Tutor.

My most vivid memory of that day is of several burly, bowler-hatted gentlemen (the College porters) dragging shut those magnificent wooden gates to prevent the crowd from following in. It was like a scene from the French Revolution.

Trinity means every modulation of light and weather, like the orange-pink glow from the stone of the Wren Library in the last rays from a wintry sun ... And the everlasting sound of photographers' boots ringing on the cobbles.

In the early morning, there is also the noise of the world coming to life beneath the window. This is something I find hard to accustom myself to, particularly the grinding noise of an Urban District Council dust lorry's engine rising and falling in spasmodic energy at seven o'clock in the morning accompanied by the jovial dustman's refrain of "O Come All Ye Faithful" and the headsplitting clang of the bins.

I've always been interested in history, even when I was quite small. I don't know whether it's me or being born into what I was, but I *feel* history. It fascinates me. I'm a romantic at heart, really.

At Gordonstoun I was very keen on it, and when the time came for me to go to Cambridge and choose my subjects, I thought, "Now here's a chance I'll never have again – to do some pre-history, and get to know about the earlier societies and the most *primitive* kinds of men."

When you meet as many people as I do, from different countries, different colours, different stages of social development with different drives, you become curious about what makes men tick, and what makes different men tick differently.

You wonder about the fundamental tension in a man, in mankind, between body and soul. I got on to this at Gordonstoun and I grabbed the chance to follow it up a bit at Cambridge.

Charles ate the 30p dinner in hall, concluding:

Trinity has the worst food in Cambridge.

His social life at college:

It's a source of great regret to me that a lot of people are frightened of what other people would think of them if they came up and talked to me.

At one of the few parties I went to in the first year, I left early because they wouldn't put on the record-player as long as I was there.

The problems of fame and recognition:

I tried using disguise once at Cambridge because I wanted to go along and see what was happening in a demonstration. I borrowed an overcoat, put up the collar and pulled down a hat over my eyes. I just looked like me trying not to look like me! And everybody kept looking.

It's the same if you put on dark glasses: everyone wonders what on earth you're doing wearing dark glasses, particularly when the sun's not out! Even if you put on a false beard, or something, it'd blow away.

I often think that the whole fun of university life is breaking the rules...

Half the fun at Cambridge is to climb in at all hours of the night. It's a great challenge and it's been going on for years. What does it really matter?

But there are other things I agree with. The guest hours have been lengthened and you can have a girl or anybody else in your room until two o'clock in the morning instead of twelve o'clock. Well, that's all right.

Student Demonstrations:

I'm not the sort of person who might march or demonstrate, no. I don't agree with violence. I'm very suspicious of mobs and mob influence...

Some of those people who've demonstrated in Grosvenor Square never went with the intention of shouting or bashing a policeman on the head, but they were amazed when they found they did.

No, I'm not a demonstrating type, unless it came to the absolute crunch and I felt this was the only way of getting something done I felt strongly about.

I can't help feeling that, because students and many people feel so helpless and so anonymous in life and society, demonstrating is one useful way of making known your own particular opinions about world affairs, domestic matters and things like that.

It may also be because it's enjoyable, a lot of other people do it, it's the thing to do, it seems to be the thing to do.

I believe that a lot of people are very serious about it, but I can't help feeling that a lot of it is purely for the sake of change, and for the sake of doing something to change things, which from my point of view is pointless. You've got to do it constructively.

Aberystwyth.

In April 1969, Charles spent a term at the University College of Wales in Aberystwyth, learning Welsh before his investiture as Prince of Wales:

Misgivings had built up, but one had an exaggerated view of the situation.

I expect at Aberystwyth there may be one or two demonstrations, and as long as

I don't get covered too much in egg and tomato, I'll be all right.

But I don't blame people demonstrating like that. They've never seen me before, they don't know what I'm like. I've hardly been to Wales and you can't really expect people to be over-zealous about having a so-called English Prince come amongst them.

I think once I've been there for eight weeks, things might improve!

I'm not an expert at heraldry and genealogy, but I'm told that I'm descended three times over from the original Welsh Princes. My grandmother, Queen Elizabeth, is descended twice over through both sides of her family, which is very interesting; and then I'm descended again on the other side. So I do have quite a lot of Welsh blood.

There was a Welsh Nationalist demonstration. Charles approached one of the demonstrators:

I had slight butterflies as I walked up, but I just went to see what it was these people were really getting at, you know? They were standing there and they were, I thought, perfectly ordinary people.

You somehow feel that, because they're demonstrating and they've got placards, they're a group apart – a sort of modern, ghastly phenomenon. Instead, I thought I might as well go and see.

So I asked one chap who was holding a placard what it was, what it meant, because it was in Welsh, and I'm afraid I haven't learnt it properly yet. So I asked him but he just hurled abuse at me, "Go home, Charlie," or something like that.

So, after I'd asked him more questions, I gave up. There was no point.

If I've learnt anything in the last eight weeks, it's been about Wales in particular, and its problems, and what these people feel about Wales. They're depressed about what might happen if they don't try to preserve the language and culture, which is unique and special to Wales. And if something is unique and special, I think it's well worth preserving.

I wouldn't have learned Welsh had I not been the Prince of Wales, but I couldn't have worked at it as hard as I did if it hadn't been another entry into history, another way to find out about people, another way of satisfying human curiosity.

I like languages very much. I can never get very far with them, because I've never had enough time to pick up much of a vocabulary, or study the constructions. But I enjoy them. I've got a good ear, and I can mimic, and I like doing it.

I worked for eight weeks on my Welsh and it was damned hard – it's a hard language, very rich and very complex – but I enjoyed it. I spent an hour and a half with my Aberystwyth tutor the other day, and he was quite pleased with how much I'd remembered, and with my accent.

GIVING A WELSH SPEECH AT ABERYSTWYTH/PHOTO RAY DANIEL

I've learnt a lot about Welsh people – and about the way they operate in Aberystwyth. In fact, to live in a small town in Wales is rather interesting. And I wouldn't have been able to do it if I hadn't gone to university like this.

I've been most touched and amazed by the reaction of the people where I've been in Aberystwyth and the surrounding countryside, as to how they welcome me. I think it's shown me a lot about the way people live, which I wouldn't have found out otherwise, remaining in Cambridge…

The Investiture.

Charles was created Prince of Wales during his time at Cheam. The announcement was made at the closing ceremony of the British & Commonwealth Games in July 1958:

I remember being acutely embarrassed when it was first announced. I heard this marvellous great cheer coming from the stadium in Cardiff, and I think for a little boy of nine it was rather bewildering. All the others turned and looked at me in amazement.

It perhaps didn't mean all that much then; later on, as I grew older, it became apparent what it meant.

Charles was formally invested as Prince of Wales at Caernarvon in July 1969:

During my investiture as Prince of Wales, I met so many people and waved so much that I woke up in the middle of the night waving my hand.

He was constantly on television at the time:

It's always me – I'm getting rather bored with my face.

Before the event:

It would be unnatural if I didn't feel any apprehension about it. I always wonder about what's going to happen in this sort of thing. But I think if I take this as it comes, it'll be much easier.

It'll be an exhausting day, but an enjoyable one, because I do enjoy ceremonies.

I don't really have the same sort of apprehension about it as the Duke of Windsor did. Perhaps one of the reasons is that I'm not as young as he was. He was only seventeen and, I think, felt very nervous and unsure of himself when he was at Dartmouth or somewhere.

He had a lot of friends of his own age, who, perhaps he felt, would take the mickey out of him because he was dressing up in pantaloons and things like that.

I don't feel so apprehensive. I'm not going to dress up as he did, and I'm older.

I look upon it, I think, as being a meaningful ceremony. I shall also be glad when it's over, because, having spent a year in the midst of controversy and talk between one side and another, it's become a friction point for many people.

Inevitably, when everybody is talking about an economic squeeze in the country, spending £250,000 on an apparently useless ceremony doesn't get

EDWARD AT HIS INVESTITURE / PHOTO POPPERFOTO

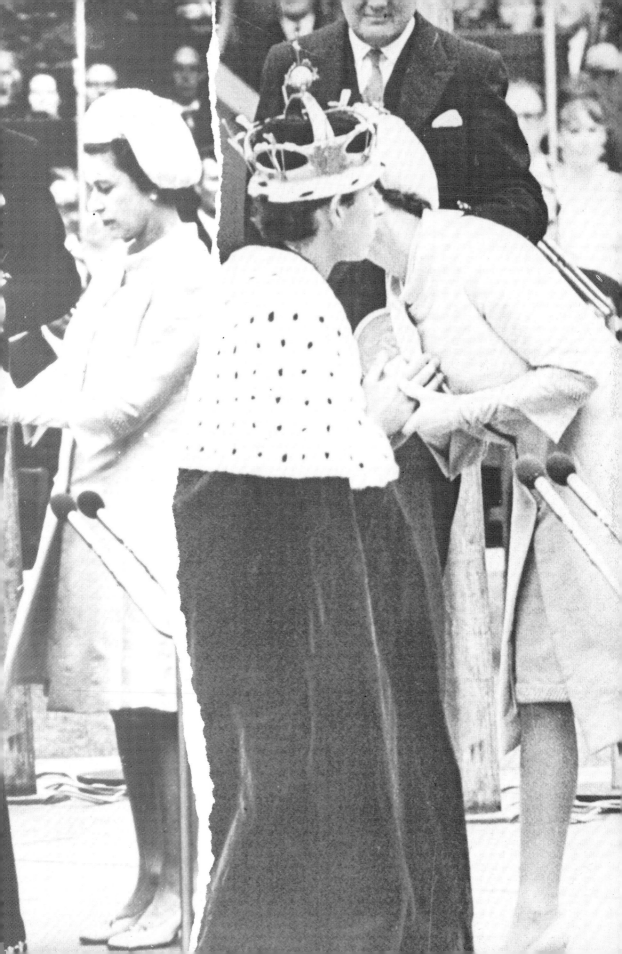

you positively anywhere, unless you think, "Oh well, we'll get some return in tourism, or investment from interested Americans."

My view of the situation is that, if you're going to have a ceremony like this, you should spend enough money to make it dignified, colourful, and worthy of Britain. But you shouldn't spend too much because it can just go on unnecessary things. On the other hand, you shouldn't spend too little because you make it skimped and you debase the whole object of the exercise.

Anybody looking at it from the outside, would wonder why on earth we went to all the bother of having a ceremony like this in an open castle, part ruin, in which there is hardly any room. If it rains we all get wet, and the Household Cavalry are having to stay in tents, in people's gardens and parks. The soldiers have to be billeted everywhere.

There is only one road and one railway into the town and the Royal train will take up the one line. I can see all the rest of the special trains will be backed-up to London!

At the ceremony the Queen and Charles exchanged the kiss of fealty:

I, Charles, Prince of Wales, do become your liege man of life and limb and of earthly worship, and faith and truth I will bear unto you to live and die against all manner of folks.

Speaking in Welsh, Charles went on to say:

The demands of a Prince of Wales have altered, but I am determined to serve and to try as best I can to live up to those demands, whatever they might be, in the rather uncertain future.

One thing I am clear about is that Wales needs to look forward without forsaking the traditions and essential aspects of her past. The past can be just as much a stimulus to the future as anything else. By the affirmation of your loyalty today, for which I express my gratitude, this will not simply be a faint hope.

The Services.

PASSING OUT PARADE AT DARTMOUTH, 1971

I'm going to be a sailor – so long as my parents will let me. (Age 11)

His plans for a career in the Royal Navy were announced while he was still at Cambridge:

I'm looking forward to it very much. I hope I shall not be too seasick.

After six months of RAF training, Charles joined the Navy in September 1971:

A period in the Services gives you great experience and responsibility: of life, of discipline, and, above all, of people and how to deal with people. To discipline them and to be disciplined by them.

It's pointless and ill-informed to say that I'm entering a profession trained in killing.

In the first place, the Services are there for fast, efficient and well-trained action in defence. Surely the Services must attract a large number of duty-conscious people? Otherwise, who else would subject themselves to being square-bashed, shouted at by petty officers and made to do ghastly things in force ten gales?

I'm entering the RAF and then the Navy because I believe I can contribute something to this country by so doing. To

RECEIVING HIS WINGS AT CRANWELL

me, it's a worthwhile occupation and one which I'm convinced will stand me in good stead for the rest of my life.

I feel that if one is going to get involved in the whole spectrum of life in this country,

WITH PRINCE PHILIP AT CRANWELL / PHOTO CENTRAL PRESS

then one should get to know about the Services. One should get to know about the Navy particularly because, ultimately, our security and everything depends upon the Navy. It always has done throughout history and always will.

I tried very hard to be as professional as possible. I hope I demonstrated a reasonable amount of enthusiasm. The difficulty was that I'd done a shortened course of introduction to the Navy and a fairly short period of training. I therefore had to try that little bit harder to assimilate the vast amount of technical information and all the navigational problems rather more quickly than other people had to do.

The trouble is that people expect me to be a genius at the very least, and to achieve the impossible rather sooner than in the immediate. I think I eventually managed to accustom myself to the pace and made people realise I couldn't necessarily live up to the programme they had mapped out.

But I think the Navy meant a great deal to me because I was basically brought up in it. My father was in it; my grandfather; my great-uncle, Lord Mountbatten; and my great-grandfathers, Prince Louis of Battenberg and King George V.

I had a very glamorous, romantic idea about it, which wasn't always borne out because there are an awful lot of mundane tasks to be carried out. But I also think the Navy's history, and the fact that it has saved this country from disaster on more than one occasion, gave me a particular interest in it, as something somebody in my position ought to know a reasonable amount about.

I hope that people in the Navy feel that I've taken an interest and can sympathise with their difficulties and aspirations.

I think it's very important that I should understand something about the defence of my country. I think the Navy ought to mean a great deal to this country – this island.

Then there is the educational value of the Services. If you want to understand what they've done for me, you can see what

they've done for thousands of other young men from every walk of life.

With the RAF of course, there was the particular bonus of flying. You have responsibilities to and for other human beings in all three Services, but most – I found, anyway – in the Navy. You're all together out there, at sea, in that small community, cut off. It's a very intense communal life.

Flying.

While in the Navy, Charles learned to fly helicopters:

I adore flying and I personally cannot think of a better combination than Navy flying – being at sea and being able to fly at the same time. I found it very exciting, very rewarding and very stimulating – also bloody terrifying, sometimes.

I think people who fly in the Fleet Air Arm are a very special breed, particularly those chaps who fly Buccaneers and Phantoms. They are taking all kinds of risks; taking off from and landing on carriers, particularly at night, is no joke.

If you're living dangerously, it tends to make you appreciate life that much more and to want to live it to the fullest. Fleet Air Arm flyers are some of the most invigorating and amusing people I've come across. I enjoyed every minute of the helicopter course at Yeovilton.

In the Queen's Flight, you tend to take off in a helicopter or aeroplane, fly in a straight line, land, get out and shake hands with a lot of people.

But at Yeovilton one did all sorts of things – commando flying, rocket firing, and landing on carriers and the back-end of ships in howling gales. I found the course easier, and got the knack more quickly than I had expected.

Many people forget that a helicopter is an inherently unstable machine. With a helicopter, you've got to expect something to go wrong any minute and be ready to do something about it pretty quickly, because if you don't, you drop like a stone. If you do make a mistake, your life often depends on taking the correct action immediately.

It's very challenging. There's that superb mixture of fear and enjoyment which comes over me.

It's marvellous when things are going right and you can pick up a reference on the ground and not bother with the map. Then that panic when you don't really know where you are and you've got to sort it out yourself. It's so exciting.

I've given myself a fright or two. The other day, we were going along quite well

when flames suddenly started to shoot out of the engine on my side, making extraordinary "whoof-whoof" noises. All the instruments were twitching away.

Fortunately, I was with the senior pilot of the squadron so we shut down the engine and landed in a ploughed field beside a motorway – much to everybody's amazement!

Part of our duties as helicopter pilots involves carrying Royal Marines. It's considered a good idea for the pilots to find out what the Marines have to put up with, from first-hand knowledge.

So I went down to do the Marines assault course at Lympstone in Devon, to do what the Marines charmingly call a "Tarzan" course – a most horrifying expedition where you have to swing over small chasms, slide down ropes at death-defying speeds and then walk across wires and up rope ladders strung between a pole and a tree. All sorts of ghastly things.

Anyway, I survived that and came out with my knees trembling in fear and trepidation. Then we had to do a form of survival course which involved crawling through tunnels half-filled with water, then running across the moor and back.

The technical side of flying was a bit of a problem:

From the flying point of view, my arithmetic is not as fast as some other peoples.

Maths taken in its pure context is misery, I think. I find it boring. I'm one of those people who prefers ideas rather than numbers. I could never understand maths. I always thought it was the way I'd been taught originally that made me so hopeless, but, on the other hand, perhaps I just don't have a mathematical mind.

HMS Bronington.

In February, 1976, Charles was given his own naval command – the mine-sweeper HMS Bronington:

It's given me a marvellous opportunity to get as close to the "ordinary" British chap as possible.

After his appointment, he told a meeting of the Grand Order of Water Rats:

If any of you are considering sailing in the North Sea next year, or if you

happen to own an oil rig in Scottish waters, I strongly advise you to increase your insurance contributions forthwith.

On being in a position of command:

One of the most important things is to be as honest and as genuine as possible. People can always see through you if you're being artificial – particularly a sailor.

And you've got to have a sense of humour, because half the battle is giving as good as you get, accepting the teasing and the ribbing.

But the most important thing about a position of responsibility or command is to get a chap to do something willingly. I know they'll moan and groan. But having done it they'll say, "That wasn't too bad, sir, was it?"

I often think there are two types of leadership. One for the more aggressive, dominant person who imposes his will forcibly on people and gains their respect through his sheer determination and

ability. The other is someone who tends to charm people and is more friendly. People feel it's worth doing something for him because they like the person.

In the summer of 1976, Charles organised a family day aboard. The invitation read:
It is hoped the trip will give a clearer idea of life at sea than can normally be extracted from your exhausted menfolk when they return home.
Charles.

AWARDING 'WINGS' TO WREN/PHOTO KEYSTONE PRESS

When nineteen-year-old Jane Chapman, Miss Spotlight of Rosyth Naval Base, came aboard, Charles welcomed her:
I presume you've taken the pill this morning. Of course, I mean the seasick pill.

HMS Bronington was the only ship in the Navy ever to make Charles seasick. He said of his first ten weeks at sea:
They took ten years off my life…
I feel about eighty.

Charles left the Navy in December, 1976:
There are other things to do and it would be rather selfish of me if I remained locked away here. It has been great fun, a splendid experience.

Sport.

PHOTO CENTRAL PRESS

I believe in living life dangerously and I think a lot of others do too.

I am a hopeless individual because I happen to enjoy an element of adventure and danger. I think that if you occasionally live dangerously it helps you appreciate life. Not only that, you discover your own abilities which, perhaps, you did not know were there.

I'm stupid enough to like trying things. I like to see if I can challenge myself to do something that is potentially hazardous, just to see if mentally I can accept that challenge and carry it out.

I like to try all sorts of things because they appeal to me. I'm one of those people who doesn't like sitting and watching someone else doing something. I don't like going to

IN A CHIPMUNK AT R.A.F. OAKINGTON/PHOTO CENTRAL PRESS

the races to watch horses thundering up and down – I'd rather be riding one myself.

Flying.

Charles made his first solo flight in January 1969:

It's imprinted on my mind indelibly. I suppose I worried about it for a bit ... the thought of actually having to go solo and whether I was capable of doing it. Whether I'd remember the right things to do.

I always thought I was going to be terrified. I was dreading the moment throughout training when I'd have to go up alone. But on the day I went solo, the instructor taxied up to the end of the runway, suddenly climbed out and said, "You're on your own, mate!"

So, there I was, and I hardly had time to get butterflies in my tummy before taking off.

I was wondering whether I could do it, but the moment I was in the air it was absolutely marvellous. There was no instructor to breathe down my neck and the aeroplane flew much better because he had gone and the weight was not there.

I had a wonderful time. I flew round and round and admired the scenery. I controlled my butterflies. Then I did a perfect landing – as it turned out, I never did a better one after that.

That had been the only thing worrying me during the flight. I had visions of going around and around until eventually the fuel ran out. But all was well.

Charles described his approach to flying:

It's a mixture between fear and supreme enjoyment. I'd like to go on flying for as long as I could but, once out of the Navy, the only flying I could do would be from one engagement to another.

I like trying my hand at things and if people say, "Do you want to have a go?", I usually say, "Yes."

He returned to Cranwell in February 1977, to brush up his flying and aerobatics:

I've forgotten so much – especially those convolutions of the stomach when you go into a roll or a loop. Dangerous? No, it's more dangerous crossing the road.

Parachuting.

Charles described his first parachute jump:

I purposely didn't think very much about the whole operation until I got into the aeroplane.

Then I did get slightly apprehensive before getting out – they say you should have butterflies. It makes you sharp, I discovered, because out I went the instant this hairy flight sergeant shouted in my ear and gave me a tap on the shoulder.

The slip-stream is terrific, particularly getting out of the side of an Andover. You appear to be flipped on your back. The next thing I knew, my feet were above my head ... which was very odd. Either I've got hollow legs or something, it doesn't often happen. The first thing I thought was, "They didn't tell me anything about this."

The next thing I knew, my legs were tangled in the rigging lines, so I was looking up at them and coming down in a

sort of U-shape. I said to myself calmly, "Your legs are in the rigging so you must remove them." So I removed them – fortunately by about 800 feet. Then I had a lovely sail down to sea level.

HIS FIRST PARACHUTE JUMP/POPPERFOTO

Of course, I forgot to inflate my life jacket because I'd enjoyed it so much. But the Royal Marines were roaring around in little rubber boats underneath and I was out of the water within ten seconds.

Diving.

Charles explored a wreck off the Virgin Islands:

There is a supreme satisfaction in life below the waves, experiencing the extraordinary sensation of swimming inside the hull of an old schooner as if it

AFTER A DIVE OFF PORTSMOUTH / PHOTO CENTRAL PRESS

THE ARCTIC / PHOTO ANWAR HUSSEIN

were some vast green cathedral filled with shoals of fish.

I can well imagine the disease which grips divers and dedicates them to their hobby or profession.

Charles dived in Arctic waters from HMS Hermes and walked upside down on a fathom of ice:

I lowered myself gingerly into the water, which by now was covered with newly formed pieces of ice – rather like Crème de menthe frappé – and sank like a

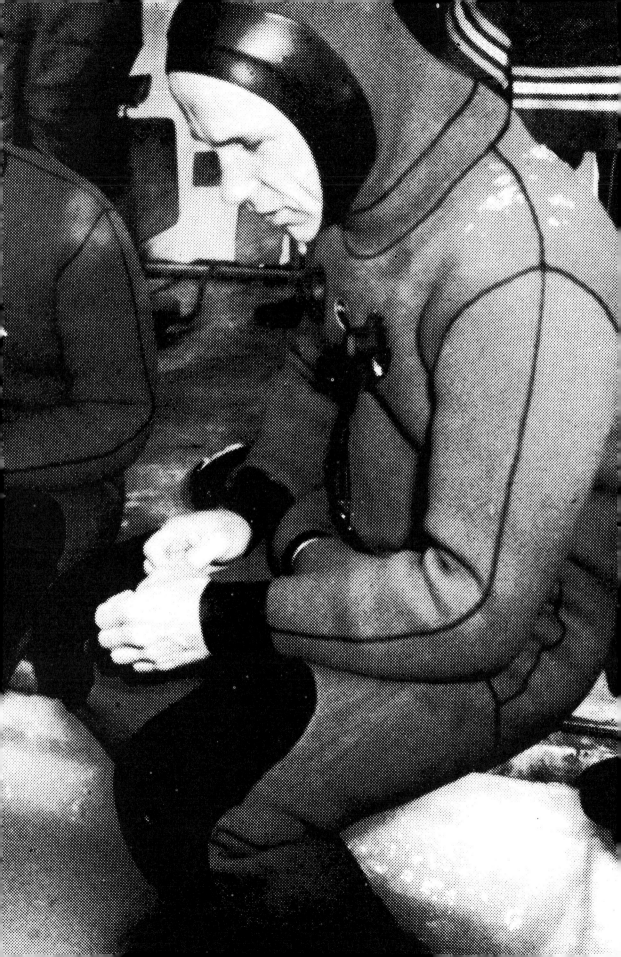

great orange walrus into the ice-covered world below.

Once at the bottom of the six-foot shaft, the similarity with a walrus vanished abruptly to be replaced by a resemblance to a dirigible balloon underwater. I found it extremely hard to preserve my balance and had to struggle to stay upright.

Despite the rubber hood, the water felt decidedly cold around my mouth and a few other edges, not to mention the fact that, with heavy gloves on my hands, I couldn't get my fingers onto my mask in order to clear my ears. So I "ballasted" myself out at a depth which was not too painful and took stock of the situation.

It was a fascinating, eerie world of greyish-greenish light that met my gaze and above all was the roof of ice which disappeared into the distance.

The visibility was extraordinarily good. The water was virtually silt-free due to the lack of wave action – the ambient light visibility was 100 feet.

I couldn't resist giving it a try! The result of my upside-down walk was highly comical in the extreme. I only partly succeeded.

What was fascinating was to see the exhaust bubbles trapped on the underside of the ice, spread out like great pools of shimmering mercury.

The icicles looked like beautiful, transparent wafers. Nestling in the gaps between the wafers were lots of shrimp-like creatures.

Other Sports.

Golf:
The game does not amuse me.

Skateboarding:
Had I known I'd have the chance to try a skateboard, I would, of course, have brought my helmet with me…

Rugger:
They always put me in the second row, the worst place in the scrum.

Surfing:
I've joined the surf club (in Wales) which is rather fun. I try to surf as often as I

can. It's a marvellous form of exercise, and you feel twice as well afterwards as before.

Ski-ing:
    We British must ski on.

PHOTO KEYSTONE

Rock Climbing:
    I don't particularly like the idea of having to cling to a rock face by the fingernails.

Polo:

I love the game, I love the ponies, I love the exercise. It's the one team game I can play. It's also a very convenient game for me as long as I spend my weekends at Windsor.

It isn't convenient to play football; you can't just nip out of Windsor Castle and enjoy a soccer game.

But if I knew that there was immense criticism of my playing polo, I'd have to think about it. You can't have everything you want, even if you feel it does no harm. People's susceptibilities count.

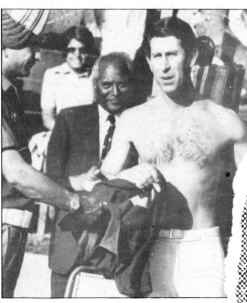

Hobbies.

CONDUCTING MOZART'S 'THE MAGIC FLUTE'/PHOTO CENTRAL PRESS

Music.

I find that music moves me very deeply. A beautiful picture, or being out on a mountain with the wind and the trees – I feel very deeply about that sort of thing.

I like music very much. I liked playing it – I haven't so much time now – and I like listening to it. The trouble is, though you haven't much time for listening, you have even less time for practising, and if you don't practise you simply can't enjoy your own noise.

When I went to prep school, I learned the piano: no good. Then I took up the trumpet. I rather enjoyed it, but one of the music teachers – who happened to be German – didn't: she couldn't stand the noise.

I used to play the trumpet in the school orchestra. We made such an awful noise, in the back row. I can hear the music teacher now. We'd all be playing away and making a hell of a din, when suddenly, she couldn't stand it any longer. She'd put down her violin, we'd all stop, and she'd shout – she had a heavy German accent and somehow, that made her sound more agonised – "Ach! Zoze trumpetz! Ach! Zoze trumpetz! Stawp Zoze Trumpetz." So I gave up the trumpet.

Later, I began to think about the 'cello. It had such a rich, deep sound. One night, I was at the Festival Hall and I heard Jacqueline Du Pré playing with her husband Daniel Barenboim. I'd never heard sounds like it. I said, "I must try this." So I did. I couldn't keep it up. I remember playing in a performance of Beethoven's Fifth one night. It was a wonderful experience, but I couldn't play concentratedly enough to avoid being confused.

Pop music I enjoy as it comes. I don't go out of my way to listen to pop sessions, but if it's there – if I happen to catch it – I enjoy it.

Whom do I like? Well, it's a bit unfair on others, because I can't always bring a name to mind when asked – particularly since I listen at random, not selectively. I like The Seekers. The Beatles sang splendid music – and wrote great music.

Jazz I enjoy. But I'm no connoisseur.

But I really prefer classical music, because I find the more I listen to classical works, the more I get out of them. Pop music may pall after two or three hearings. The Beatles were an exception for me: the more I heard them, the more I enjoyed them.

In classical music my taste, such as it is, is conservative: Bach, Mozart and Beethoven. But there are exceptions, such as Berlioz.

Once, I was listening to Richard Baker's 'These You Have Loved,' on the BBC. He played a piece by Berlioz from a choral work I'd never heard of: 'L'enfance du Christ.' I thought, "I must get it." I play it now, often. There's a certain passage in it which is so moving I'm reduced to tears every time.

I'm not mad keen on much modern music. I love *tunes,* and I love *rhythm.* Rhythm is deep in me – if I hear rhythmic music I just want to get up and dance. That's one of the reasons why I had such a marvellous time in the West Indies.

A good deal of modern music is tuneless, as far as I'm concerned. But it can grow on you with familiarity. For instance, once I sang in Benjamin Britten's *Saint Nicholas,* and I didn't appreciate it at all at first. After several rehearsals, I began to enjoy it.

The same tended to be true with the *Dream of Gerontius,* in which I also sang while at school and in the choir. I now become intensely moved by listening to it.

Have you ever sung in a big choir?

It's marvellous. I sang in the Bach 'B Minor Mass' – there's nothing like it. I don't know whether it's the volume of the voices, or the sense of participation – you're not just listening, you're helping to make the sound – but it's really very exciting.

But it's something you can enjoy only if you keep at it. You can't just turn up and say, "I like singing in choirs. Can I sing in yours tonight, please?"

One of the things I really enjoy about being Patron of the Royal Opera is having the chance to see as many operas as I can and to find out more about it.

I like to think I can go whenever I want to, at short notice – turfing people out of the Royal Box so I can get a seat!

Painting.

I'm one of those people who leaps from one thing to another. I took up water-colour painting about two years ago. It's frightfully difficult. I tried to get some lessons from Edward Seago who was a great Norfolk painter. He died, sadly, last year. He'd never given lessons in his life. He said, "All right. I'll give you a lesson, but only one."

I just sat and watched in awe as he proceeded to paint a picture entirely from memory. Before you could say "knife," in fifteen minutes, there was this marvellous little picture of two Thames barges. I said, "Can I have it?" and he said, "Of course."

I'm going to take more lessons. It's very rewarding, very hard work. And marvellous for Christmas presents!

Theatre.

I enjoy very much going to the theatre and to concerts when I can. The quality of plays and the music is astonishingly good. I do think London has extremely high standards and is one of the great cultural centres of the world, one of the great theatrical centres.

Of course, one could easily say that one's own country has the best of everything. But I think in this case it's probably true.

I love, as I say, going to the theatre because I rather enjoy acting and therefore I like live entertainment.

I enjoy films as well. But there's a special atmosphere to the theatre. I like going out

to enjoy a good laugh, but I have to watch who I take because their name inevitably appears in the papers!

I went to see a thing called *Absurd Person Singular.* I thought it extremely funny; very slick and fast. I'd never heard of Mr. Alan Ayckbourn. I hadn't seen any of his plays before. I believe he's also got another one on, called *The Norman Conquests.*

I was sad to see, when I went, that there were very few people in the theatre. I suppose it was the wrong night or something, but it was my birthday, and I thought it would be fun to take the Queen and Princess Alexandra out to the theatre.

Television.

Very much a question of time. It's weeks since I had a night on my own. I've had some very interesting evenings in and out of the Palace in the past few weeks, but not one when I could say to myself, "I'll have a look at a TV programme."

When I do get a chance, I love watching selected things. But I find television a great drug and, before you know where you are, you just sit there with your eyes becoming square and everybody saying, "Oh, come on, we'll watch it a bit longer."

There are some things I love watching like Monty Python, The Goodies, or certain documentaries.

The other night there was a programme on how birds navigate thousands of miles across oceans. It was most intriguing. Those sort of programmes are marvellous, but there's an awful lot of tripe.

Films.

Charles saw an X-film, 'Percy's Progress,' while staying in Cornwall, causing much press comment:

It was frightfully funny. There were about twelve people in the cinema – two courting couples and some other curious characters.

I think it just happened because we were in the Duchy of Cornwall area; that added to the chances of publicity.

Everybody recognised me instantly in the pubs. Marvellous old boys in caps came up and said, "Like ter shake yer hand." They were charming. One old boy produced his Home Guard certificate, signed by my grandfather.

But that sort of thing never gets reported. It's all this business about looking for scrumpy. Everybody must think I'm an alcoholic.

I mean, I don't go to these things for serious reasons. At the time of the Okehampton incident, we were on an exercise in the middle of Dartmoor. The tent was sopping wet and everybody decided to go off. What would have been the point of my being stand-offish and saying, "I'm not going to the pub, I'm not going to the cinema." As it happens, it wasn't even a blue movie.

Acting.

Charles made his acting début while at Cambridge:

I spent many hours with a tape recorder listening to a long soliloquy of Richard Hunchback spoken by Sir Laurence before taking this on myself.

I must have been either incredibly good or absolutely appalling, because

PHOTO CENTRAL PRESS

acting techniques – I mean timing and double entendres and everything are enormously helpful.

I enjoy making people laugh if I can and I always believe humour is a very useful way of getting people to listen to what you are saying.

In a sketch written by himself, Charles came onstage with an umbrella:
I lead a sheltered life.

Reading.

I have a congenital defect, which is being unable to remain awake for very long once I sit down with a book. But I do love reading very much and used to do a lot of it when I was at sea and had more time.

I tend to read a lot of history and a lot of biographies.

I'm fascinated by some of the books of Alexander Solzhenitsyn. I found 'The Gulag Archipelago' riveting, utterly horrifying and most moving.

Many people accused Solzhenitsyn of exaggeration, and maintained things were not nearly as bad as he made out. There will always be people like that.

Personally, I doubt that Solzhenitsyn is exaggerating when he talks about a decline in courage being possibly the most striking feature which an outside observer notices in the West in our days.

It does indeed seem as though one of the great abiding problems of Western society is the lack of individual courage of the sort that can withstand the fashionable attitudes of the pressures of collectivism.

According to Solzhenitsyn, we operate at the extreme limits of the legal framework of our societies, and he criticises the situation, saying, "Whenever the tissue of life is woven of legalistic relations there is an attitude of moral mediocrity paralysing man's noblest attitudes."

It's clear, I think, that we've neglected the moral factor in man. Karl Marx assumed that the goodness of man would assert itself automatically when the economic changes had been achieved.

when I finished there was a stunned silence from the parents until the producer in the wings started some applause.

In many places the facilities for amateur and professional acting are either non-existent or a disgrace to the community. Drama is just as important as gleaming new bingo halls, if not more so.

I can't help feeling it is an element of frustration and boredom which creates some of the uncivilised and uncouth reaction in present society and perhaps the theatre can absorb some of the frustration.

The Government is more than justified in spending money on the dramatic arts, and I hope they will continue to go on doing so.

To my regret, when I leave Cambridge the opportunities for acting, for crouching in uncollected dustbins and receiving custard pies in an ecclesiastical face, will be limited.

I love imitating and mimicking. I enjoyed acting enormously at school and university. In a strange way, so much of what one does requires acting ability one way or another and I enjoy it.

For instance, if you are making a speech it is extremely useful if you can use

But he didn't see that a better society couldn't be brought into life by people who hadn't undergone a moral change within themselves.

I think it's essential to consider the human aspects, and to examine industrial society from the standpoint of what it does to the human qualities of man, to his soul and his spirit.

Writing.

Charles made his début as a book reviewer by reviewing Harry Secombe's novel 'Twice Brightly' for Punch:

It is a compendium of Welsh wit and thespianism.

I am hopelessly biased in favour of the works of Ned of Wales. I have always been an ardent supporter of this particular Welshman.

Reading the book, I was shaken with spasms of mirth at frequent intervals.

It reeks of the theatre, conjures up the excitement, the sheer knee-trembling terror of a first appearance on stage.

Charles loved The Goons and wrote an introduction to a volume of 'Goon Show' scripts:

It has always been one of my profound regrets that I was not born ten years earlier, since I would then have had the pure, unbounded joy of listening avidly to the Goons each week.

Instead, I only discovered that the Goon-type humour appealed to me just as the shows were drawing to a close. Then, I discovered 'The Ying Tong Song' in record form and, almost at once, I knew it by heart – the only song I do know by heart.

I plagued everybody with its dulcet tones and 'Solo For Raspberry Blower' to such an extent that when my small brothers heard a recording of the Goons for the first time they thought it was their elder brother!

It must be such hell writing a book. They are so *long,* aren't they?

Travel.

The whole idea of these visits is for me to meet as many people as I can, so they can see for themselves that I'm a pretty ordinary sort of person and not different from anyone else.

I hope that if I do go abroad, I can combine it with visiting various places and being a kind of ambassador.

My idea of a holiday is to do all the things I can't do when I'm not on holiday.

Many people think of a holiday as an occasion on which to lie down, go to sleep and do absolutely nothing. I like going off and being energetic, running around in circles and generally appearing absolutely mad.

I like going off somewhere really wild and seeing it before it has lodges built all over it.

Australia:

A funny thing happened to me on my way to Australia – I made a mistake and got off the plane.

The Australians:

They were very, very good and marvellous people. Very genuine, and said exactly what they thought. The only person who took the mickey out of me, or

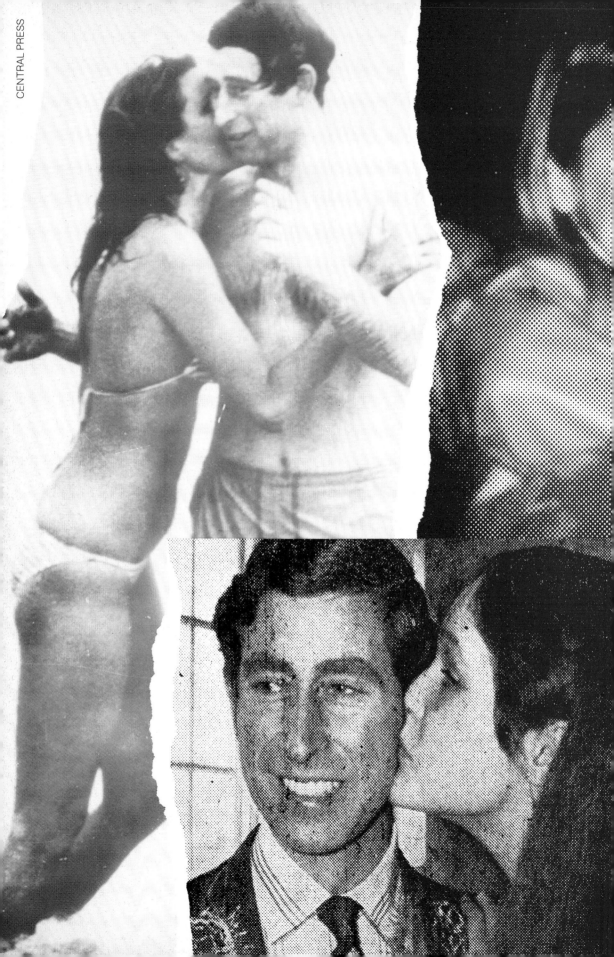

made me feel at all unhappy, I think, was an Englishman . . . very strange, but that was the only time.

Except on another occasion when I went into the unit one evening and I had an umbrella with me – it had been raining quite heavily – and they all looked rather quizzically at this strange, English thing. As I walked out having turned the lights off, there were marvellous shouts of, "Oh, Pommy Bastard."

But that was about the only time the Australians ever took the mickey out of me, I think.

Arriving in Canberra in 1977:
I would like to meet as many people as possible during my stay, and this does not exclude eligible young ladies.

On renaming Brisbane's Chermside Hospital, Prince Charles Hospital:

I look forward to returning one day and naming it something else.

In the gold-mining city of Bendigo, huge crowds waited to see him:
It looks as though you have emptied out some of the pubs. However, I trust you won't waste good drinking time once I've gone into the town hall.

Charles first visited Papua during his first term at Timbertop in January 1966:
I can't help feeling that less and less interest is being taken by the younger Papuans in the customs and skills of their parents and grandparents. They feel that they have to live up to European standards and that these things belong to the past and have no relevance to the present or future.

This may be a completely false impression, but I was given one or two presents by young people and when I

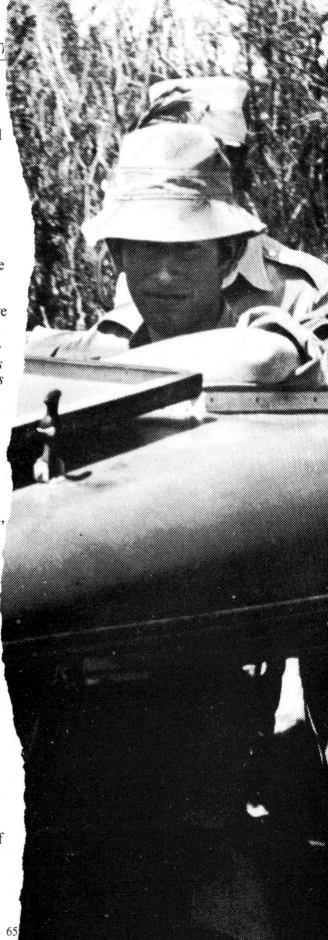

asked them if they had made them, they said their mothers or aunts had.

But I expect there will always be those who make souvenirs for tourists. If not, I hope a suitable amount of relics will be preserved for history.

I would like to mention how fresh and sincere I found the church at Dogura. Everyone was so eager to take part in the services, and the singing was almost deafening. One felt it might almost be the original church.

Where Christianity is new, it must be much easier to enter into the spirit of it wholeheartedly, and it is rather wonderful that you can still go somewhere where this strikes you.

Charles returned to Papua in 1975 for their independence ceremony. One of the islands was threatening to break away and Charles advised by quoting St. Paul's Epistle to the Romans:

"Everyone must obey the State authorities, for no authority exists without God's permission, and the existing authorities have been put there by God.

"Whoever opposes the existing authority opposes what God has ordered, and anyone who does so will bring judgement on himself."

Charles visited Bermuda in October 1970, as part of the island's celebration of 350 years of parliamentary government:

Bearing in mind that I am the first Charles to have anything to do with a Parliament for 350 years, I might have turned nasty and dissolved you.

Charles visited the Gilbert & Ellice Islands when they became independent. He was serving on the frigate Minerva at the time.

I am delighted to be here to escape from the clutches of my senior officers.

Charles and Anne visited Kenya on safari in February 1971:

That was something I really enjoyed. It was the best thing I've ever done, or one of the best – the sort of enlightened masochism which I go in for. The fun of it is one could really walk about the bush

and come across animals suddenly and watch them.

The game scouts all thought I was absolutely mad, being in a dried-up piece of country instead of sitting in hotels and letting the animals come to me.

The first rhino seen is always a very exciting thing because they are prehistoric, primeval creatures and this one was just sort of standing there churning up the dust. Then it came closer and we were trying to see if we could get it to come closer still or perhaps charge us. But it didn't.

Visiting the Alhambra in Granada, 1972:
It's so marvellous, I can't understand why tourists don't take it away stone by stone.

Visiting Nassau in July 1973:
It provided me with the opportunity to discover the peace and fascination of life on a Bahamian beach – something I'd never experienced before and which gave me great happiness and contentment. That is, until I discovered those proverbial grains of sand wedged between the royal toes. So, you see, I carry a piece of the Bahamas with me now wherever I go.

Visiting Malta:
I am told many Maltese believe my future appearance was determined whilst my parents were on this island.

Driving a team of huskies in Canada:
That just sleighed me.

Eating raw seal meat with Eskimos:
For the honour of the family, I picked up a piece of meat and made the fatal error, of course, of chewing it rather than swallowing it like a sheep's eye. The trouble is that it tasted absolutely appalling.

I said, "The Press here are going to eat this, and all the people with me . . . you'll all eat it." They shrank away and disappeared.

A doctor who was with us muttered in their ears that they shouldn't eat it because it was probably a week old. So I said, "Thank you very much chummy, what about me, eh?!"

While in Canada, Charles dressed in Caribou fur:
I hope we don't meet a polar bear because he might think I'm in season.

Eskimos protested when Charles said:
I must be very careful as to whose nose I rub.

Charles later apologised:
I suppose it was a bad joke, a bad cliché. I hope I didn't give offence.

Zaire, 1979:
It was pouring with rain when I arrived at the airport. They had a guard of honour drawn up and they were absolutely soaked, poor things. I don't know why they didn't move them into a hangar. Next morning when I left, they were still there, soaked to the skin.

Ivory Coast, 1977:
Please be indulgent if I massacre the French language. I hope I may have the opportunity to find, perhaps, a brilliant Ivorian female teacher.

After spending several days in the Himalayan foothills of Nepal, 1980:
It was great fun. Each village turned out to greet us – everyone was so welcoming.

It was marvellous to wake up in the morning, open the tent window and see the mountains framed like a picture.

After hiking in the mountains:
Do I look disgusting enough? I'm not tired. I could still go on for three or four days.

India, November 1980:
As you know, in Britain we have welcomed many of your relatives.

During the same visit:
May the udders of your buffaloes be always full of milk.

Visiting the Taj Mahal, he was asked if he was touched by it:
Well, I did bang my head against the ceiling at one point.

Describing the Taj Mahal to the BBC:
A marvellous idea, to build something so wonderful . . . to someone one loved so much.

Speaking with an Indian actress in Bombay about her latest film:
    Are there any bed scenes? No kissing either, I suppose.

About a girl he met in Texas in 1977:
    I told her I'd like to make a sporting tour of America. She said to me, "Indoors or outdoors?" My reply is not on record.

BOMBAY, 1980 / PHOTO KEYSTONE PRESS

WITH MRS. GANDHI IN NEW DELHI / KEYSTONE

On millionaires in Texas:
      I thought about all those daughters.
Oil wells are very valuable as dowry.

*At a star-studded dinner in Hollywood,
with Dean Martin, Cary Grant and
Charlie's Angels:*
      I'm horrified to speak on matters
I know so little about. Nerves are
overcoming me. Perhaps I can borrow
Cary Grant's teeth – they might fit me
better than him.

*He was seated between Angie Dickinson
and Farrah Fawcett-Majors:*
      It's been an amazingly enjoyable
evening, sitting between two of the most
beautiful cops I've ever met. I only wish it
were possible to arrange a swop with some
of my policemen. I've been trying to
persuade them to do that for years, but
they won't agree.

Family, Friends & Others.

The Royal Family:
It's like living in a glass-house.

I'm very lucky because I have very wise and incredibly sensible parents who have created a marvellous, secure, happy home.

I believe that the family unit is the most important aspect of our particular society. Above all else, it ensures that the majority of people are subject to an influence and an atmosphere of love, security – sanctions if you like – which are individual, rather than State-orientated.

I think the moment the family unit breaks down, it increases the chance of totalitarianism coming into operation.

I think, inevitably, some discipline is needed for children, and I think a lot of people expect somebody else to do the disciplining for them. I know I needed discipline.

If being old-fashioned means fostering a good family atmosphere, then I'm proud to be old-fashioned and will certainly remain so.

We are a family of human beings, not a set of symbols, and I think everybody would want us to be real.

I think of my family as very special people. I've never wanted not to have a home life – to get away from home. I love my home

73

life. We happen to be a very close-knit family. I'm happier at home with my family than anywhere else.

I find I'm becoming a bit more independent. I think I may be slightly late in developing. I'm not sure.

His mother, the Queen:
 She is just a marvellous person and a wonderful mother.

His father, Prince Philip:
 He lets one get on with what you want to do. He gives one the opportunity to do these things. He says: "We think it might be an idea; what do you think?" In that sense, he's been an influence – but a moderating influence and an influence of great wisdom.

PHOTO CENTRAL PRESS

Charles and Philip no longer sail together:

I remember one disastrous day when we were racing and my father was, as usual, shouting. We wound the winch harder and the sail split in half with a sickening crack. Father was not pleased.

Not long after that, I was banned from the boat after an incident cruising in Scotland: There was no wind and I was amusing myself taking potshots at beer cans floating round the boat. The only gust of the day blew the jib in front of my rifle just as I fired. I wasn't invited back on board.

I'm often asked whether it's because of some generic trait that I stand with my

hands behind my back, like my father. The answer is that we both have the same tailor – he makes the sleeves so tight that we can't get our hands in front.

The Queen Mother:

Ever since I can remember, my Grandmother has been the most wonderful example of fun, laughter, warmth, infinite security and, above all else, exquisite taste in so many things.

For me, she will always be one of those extraordinary, rare people whose touch can turn everything to gold – whether it be putting people at their ease, turning something dull into something

amusing, bringing happiness and comfort to people, or making any house she lives in a unique haven of cosiness and character.

Prince Andrew:
Ah, the one with the Robert Redford looks?

Lord Mountbatten:
He is a unique personality. In a way, he is the modern-day equivalent of Queen Victoria in relation to the family. He has the amazing ability to get on with everybody in the family.

He knows more about my immense family than anybody else. He has written relationship tables: he knows who everybody's related to as far back as . . . Charlemagne, on his side!

He also has an amazing ability for giving good advice, for sound reason, sensible and wise opinions about all things.

People love him because he is incredibly honest, straightforward, and doesn't mind what he says at all, to anybody and never has done from the year dot.

He is, I think, the centre of the family, the last person of his generation that knew everybody. He was brought up to think very strongly that the family was an important concept, which I feel very deeply too.

Certainly, Lord Mountbatten has had an influence on my life and I admire him, I think, almost more than anybody else. He's a very great person.

After Mountbatten was murdered:
I adored him – and miss him so dreadfully now.

It is a cruel and bitter irony that he should have survived two world wars and then be blown to bits by sub-human extremists.

He had that quality of real moral courage, of being able to tackle unpleasant tasks. That, in these days, is a rare quality indeed. He had it in abundance.

Prince Louis of Battenberg:
Pride swells when I recall the part played by my great-grandfather in the formation of the Royal Naval Air

WITH LORD MOUNTBATTEN

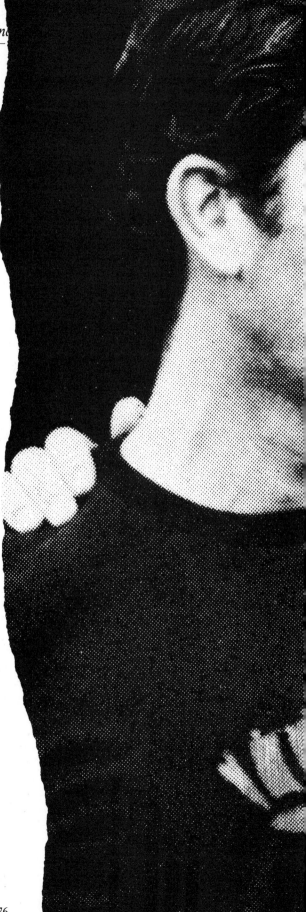

Squadron in 1914. Without his interest and enthusiasm, and his determined support of the aeroplane versus the airship, the Naval Air Service might quite literally have had great difficulty in getting off the ground.

Charles I:
I realised that Charles I was not entirely splendid and innocent, as I had always thought.

His ancestor, King George III:
I think I first got interested because people have gone on for years and years in the history books describing him as the

"mad Monarch." If you ask any school child, I'll bet you what he says about George III is that he was mad.

I felt that he was a much-maligned monarch – particularly by American historians who obviously found it convenient to blame him to a certain extent, to make it easier to justify the American Revolution. They could argue they were revolting against a mad monarch who had no credibility in America.

His so-called madness, in the light of modern medical knowledge and research, may in fact have resulted from a physical

disease, a condition of the blood known as porphyria. This actually makes you appear demented occasionally; it goes in cycles.

He was a great patron of the arts, and a great patron of scientific development in the 18th century.

I admire him enormously for what he did and for his incredible capacity for hard work and conscientious devotion to duty.

A lot of people would regard this as boring because he didn't do what Charles II reportedly did and have affairs with all sorts of delectable ladies. That's always much more glamorous than a chap who works hard and is a conscientious monarch – and is also more discreet!

His friends:

I tend to have a few, but very good friends. I always rather fought shy, at school and elsewhere, of group or gang behaviour. I've always been happier with one or two people. I do have some marvellous friends – I'm very lucky. I've made them since I left school. I've just got one or two friends left that I knew at school.

I trust my friends implicitly, and they know that. The more discreet, the better. Those people who do get drawn into conversations and do natter about me find they get into the papers. But I hear they don't get paid very much. Five pounds, or two pounds. Or is it ten with inflation?

I do have friends outside a narrow circle; it's a different type of friendship. A person's closest friends, whatever his position, are determined by his interests and way of life. For instance, I enjoy shooting: therefore, I see a lot of people who shoot. A number of them are "members of the aristocracy." Not all. But it isn't that they are landed gentry which is the *cause* of my seeing them. It's shooting.

On the other hand, when I was at Cambridge, I got to know some very different kinds of people. One man in particular comes to mind, and he's an academic. We write to each other, but we don't meet as often as we did because he's in the North of England and I'm down

CHARLES MEETS SIR WINSTON CHURCHILL / PHOTO CENTRAL PRESS

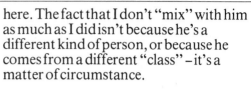

here. The fact that I don't "mix" with him as much as I did isn't because he's a different kind of person, or because he comes from a different "class" – it's a matter of circumstance.

Winston Churchill:
His recorded words still cause a tingle to run up and down my spine and bring a tear to my eye. He was able to use words the way Mozart used musical notes.

There is a loch in the grounds called Loch Muick which we used to net for trout. I've never forgotten seeing him seated on a rock in the loch with an enormous tree trunk across his knees saying, "I am waiting for the Loch Muick monster."

Frank Sinatra:
Sinatra could be terribly nice one minute, and, well, not so nice, the next. I was not impressed with the creeps and mafia types he kept around him.

WITH TRICIA NIXON/PHOTO JAMES PICKERELL, CAMERA PRESS

Tricia Nixon:
Artificial and plastic.

Julie Nixon:
A bright, warm personality.

Love & Marriage.

WITH LADY DIANA AND PRINCESS GRACE/PHOTO CENTRAL PRESS

A lot of people, I feel, have a false idea about love. I think it's more than just a romantic idea of falling madly in love with someone and having a love affair for the rest of your life. It's much more than that: it's a very strong friendship.

As often as not, you have shared interests and ideas in common, plus a great deal of affection. You are very lucky when you find someone who attracts you in the physical, as well as the mental sense.

Obviously, there must be someone, somewhere for me.

When you get to my extraordinary stage of decrepitude, you begin to think about things like that, as I'm sure you know. You look at a girl and think, "I wonder if one could ever marry her," or something like that.

And obviously, there are certain people I've thought of on those lines.

In many cases, one falls madly in "love" with somebody with whom you are infatuated rather than in love.

I hope I will be as lucky as my own parents who have been so happy.

His Ladies.

It's very hard on them, I have layers to protect me, but they are not used to it. It tends, sometimes, to put the really nice

ones off. Poor Jane Wellesley; I am shielded, but how can she be protected?

Lady Jane Wellesley:
There was also that marvellous theory that the reason for Princess Anne's marriage was to allow me to conduct my operations under cover. Of course, nothing transpired.

But as you know, only too well, the great problem as a result of my sister announcing her engagement, having said only a few months previously that there was no truth in the rumours is that the Press, I know, will never, ever again, believe it if you say there is no truth and we're just good friends!

Princess Caroline of Monaco:
I have only met the girl once and they are trying to marry us off.

Princess Marie-Astrid:
If I marry a Catholic, I'm dead. I've had it.

Marriage.

Referring to Edward VIII:
I will not become a martyr to the cause.

Whenever I give a dinner party these days, more and more of the people seem to be married.

Marriage is a much more important business than falling in love. I think one must concentrate on marriage being essentially a question of mutual love and respect for each other.

Creating a secure family unit in which to bring up children, to give them a happy, secure upbringing – that's what marriage is all about, creating a home.

Essentially, you must be good friends, and love, I'm sure, will grow out of that friendship.

I have a particular responsibility to ensure that I make the right decision. The last thing I could possibly entertain is getting divorced.

I've fallen in love with all sorts of girls and I fully intend to go on doing so. But, I've made sure I haven't married the first person I've fallen in love with.

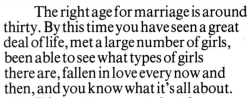

The right age for marriage is around thirty. By this time you have seen a great deal of life, met a large number of girls, been able to see what types of girls there are, fallen in love every now and then, and you know what it's all about.

I'd never recommend getting married too young. You miss so much, you get tied down.

I certainly won't get married until I've left the Navy. I couldn't cope with both. It would be too difficult a problem, and I think it's very unfair on a woman to be continually left behind. I'd rather wait until I could supply as much company as possible, particularly in the first years of marriage.

I like to think I've watched other people. Having tried to learn from other people's experiences, other people's mistakes – yes, in one's own family and in other people's – I hope I shall be able to make a reasonable decision and choice.

The more industrialised and artificial our lives become, the more standards tend to fall. I think one of the reasons the divorce rate goes up is because people no longer feel that marriage is important.

You have to remember that when you marry in my position, you're going to marry someone who, perhaps, is one day going to be queen. You've got to choose somebody very carefully, I think, who could fulfil this particular role, and it has got to be somebody pretty unusual.

The one advantage about marrying a princess, for instance, or somebody from a royal family, is that they do know what happens.

The only trouble is that I often feel I'd like to marry somebody English, or, perhaps, Welsh. Well, British anyway.

To me, marriage – which may be for fifty years – seems to be one of the biggest and most responsible steps to be taken in one's life. Which makes it all sound hideously complicated.

My marriage has to be for ever. It's sad, in a way, that some people should feel that there is every opportunity to just break it off when you feel like it. I mean, the whole point about the marriage contract was that it was for life.

And marriage isn't only for the two people who form the marriage; it's also for the children of that marriage.

Presumably, in the first place, the institution of marriage was started in order to allow children to have a reasonable degree of security in their upbringing so that they became reasonable and responsible human beings. But if they were the children of people who simply dashed from one place to another with different people all the time, they'd turn into the most extraordinary individuals – as happens only too often.

LADY DIANA

LADY JANE WELLESLEY

LADY SARAH SPENCER, DIANA'S SISTER

If you feel you can change it, change your mind and try anybody else at the drop of a hat, then that's sad. Marriage is something you ought to work at. I may easily be proved wrong, but I certainly intend to work at it when I get married.

Whatever your place in life, when you marry you're forming a partnership which you hope will last, say, fifty years. I certainly hope so, because I've been brought up in a close-knit, happy family, and family life means more to me than anything else. So I'd want to marry somebody who had interests which I understood and could share.

Then look at it from the woman's point of view. A woman not only marries a man, she also marries into a way of life, into a job, into a life in which she's got a contribution to make. She's got to have some knowledge of it, some sense of it, or she wouldn't have a clue about whether she's going to like it. If she didn't have a clue, it would be too risky for her, wouldn't it?

If I'm deciding on whom I want to live with for the next fifty years – well that's the last decision in which I'd want my head to be ruled entirely by my heart. It's nothing to do with class; it's to do with compatibility.

There are as many cases of marriages turning out unsatisfactorily because a man married above himself as there are

SABRINA GUINNESS

ANNA WALLACE

DAVINA SHEFFIELD

LADY AMANDA KNATCHBULL

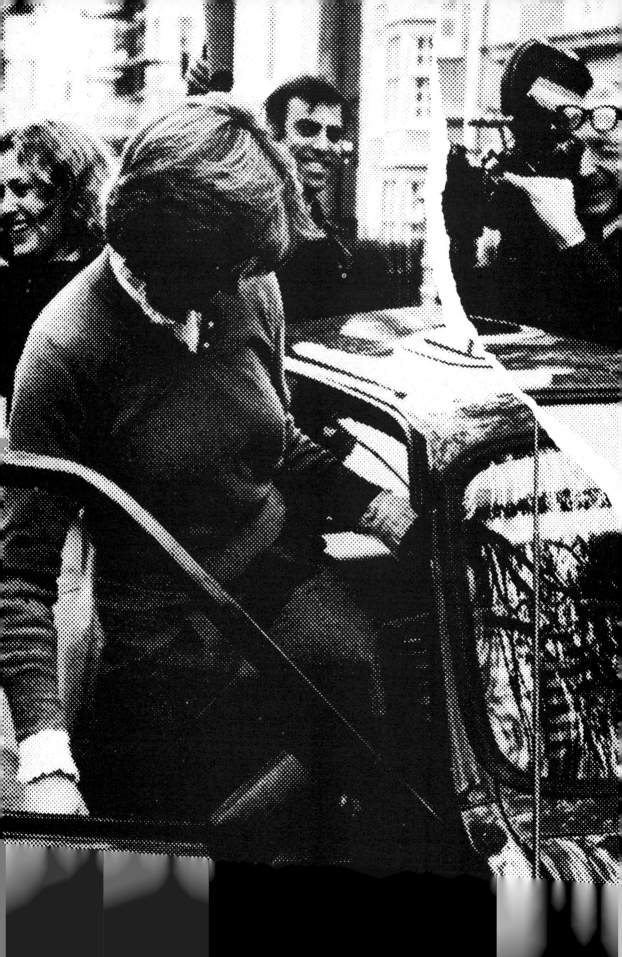

CHEVENING HOUSE IN KENT / PHOTO A. F. KERSTING

when he married below. Marriage isn't an "up" or "down" issue anyway: it's a side-by-side one.

Lady Diana.

Diana was an old friend of the family. Charles remembered:

What a very amusing and jolly – and attractive – sixteen-year-old she was.

Diana is a real outdoor-loving sort of person.

Diana is a great skier.

They were together at Balmoral during July 1980:

I began to realise what was going on in *my* mind and hers in particular.

Charles confided to an aide during his walking tour in the Himalayas:

I'm terrified of getting it wrong.

Charles proposed over dinner for two in his third-floor quarters at Buckingham Palace before Diana went to Australia:

I wanted to give Diana a chance to think about it – to think if it all was going to be too awful.

She'd planned to go to Australia quite a long time before anyway, with her mother, and I thought, "Well, I'll ask her then so that she'll have a chance of thinking it over while she's away and saying, 'I can't bear the whole idea' – or not, as the case may be."

After his proposal was accepted:

I feel positively delighted and frankly amazed that Di is prepared to take me on.

Their honeymoon:

We've discussed vague ideas and now people might come up with suggestions of where we might go.

The difference between their ages:

I haven't somehow thought about it. I mean, it's only twelve years and lots of people have got married with that sort of age difference. I just feel you are as old as you think you are.

Charles On Himself.

I tend to be a jack-of-all-trades.

Were it not for my ability to see the funny side of my life, I'd have been committed to an institution long ago.

David Frost asked him how he'd describe himself:
Sometimes, a bit of a twit.

The most important quality a person like myself needs is a sense of humour and the ability to laugh at oneself.

When we've been talking at sea, some of the sailors say, "Wouldn't you like to have a life of your own? Wouldn't you like to be able to go down to the pub?" Well, I *have* got a life of my own, and I like it. Life doesn't consist of going down to the pub. The pleasure in life consists of going down to the pub if that's what you like to do.

And I do quite as much of what I like to do as is good for me, and I do a lot of other things which are work, just as everybody else has to work. Sometimes the sailors said, "Wouldn't you like to be free?" Free from what? Being free isn't doing what other people like to do, it's doing what *you* like to do.

I'm not a rebel by temperament. I don't get a kick out of not doing what is expected of me, or of doing what is not expected of me. I don't feel an urge to react against older people. I've been brought up with older people and I've enjoyed it. And now that I'm twenty-five, other people's ages don't matter anyway.

Occasionally you have to stick your neck out.

I was asked whether I concentrated on developing my "image" – as if I was some kind of washing powder, presumably with a special blue whitener. I have absolutely no idea what my image is and therefore I intend to go on being myself to the best of my ability.

I dare say that I could improve my image in some circles by growing my hair to a more fashionable length, being seen at the Playboy Club at frequent intervals, and squeezing myself into tight clothes.

I dare say many of my views and beliefs would be considered old-fashioned and out of date. But that doesn't worry me... Fashion, by its very definition, is transitory; human nature being what it is, what was old-fashioned at length becomes in fashion. Thus the whole process continues.

I don't believe in fashion, full stop. I admit I am pretty square. I couldn't care less.

Yes, I think one can be normal if one starts being an international personality right from the word go.

I'm not a normal person in the sense that I was born to be king. I've received a special education and training. I could never be a normal person because I've been prepared to reign over my subjects.

While making a speech, he touched on the problems of public speaking:
I can tell you that writing speeches is a major sweat. Actually sitting down and thinking is a sweat. Worrying whether you're going to say the right thing is another problem, of course, because everybody will jump on you.

You have no idea, ladies and gentlemen, what excruciating suffering you have caused, what intense intellectual effort has been expended upon this oration involving innumerable man hours at a negative rate of overtime. Life, I can assure you, is tough at the top!

My profession is somewhat indefinable and so I find myself holding forth on subjects about which I know very little for far too long.

My views change and my outlook evolves as I grow older, and I deeply resent being attributed with views I expressed as a younger, and less wise man.

The problem is to get through a certain amount of anxiety or nervousness or prejudice, or whatever to start with. It usually takes about twenty minutes . . .

they're maybe beginning to realise that you're vaguely human and then you've got to go.

I'm still fairly shy. One just has to conquer this. It's one of those things that comes as you grow older.

I don't make friends all that easily. Perhaps the position that one is in builds up a little bit of a barrier, but I find now that I'm making more friends.

The time to get anxious, in a way, is when nobody's interested at all.

Many people are too shy and overcome in the presence of royalty. Only the dignitaries seem to talk to me on well-tried subjects, usually of little interest.

Unfortunately the nicest people are those who won't come up and make themselves known. They're terrified of being seen to be friendly in case they'll be accused of sucking-up or because they imagine, quite wrongly, that I won't want to talk to them.

I used to think, "Good God, what's wrong? Do I smell? Have I forgotten to change my socks?" I realise now that I have to make a bit of the running and show that I'm a reasonable human being. An awful lot of people say eventually, "Good Lord, you're not nearly as pompous as I thought you were going to be."

The Monarchy.

THE QUEEN MOTHER AND FAMILY ON HER BIRTHDAY/PHOTO CENTRAL PRESS

One of the oldest professions in the world.

I maintain that the greatest function of any monarchy is the human concern which its representatives have for the people, especially in what is becoming an increasingly inhuman era – an age of computers, machines, multi-national organisations. This, to my mind, is where the future can be promising.

In these times, the monarchy is called into question – it's not to be taken for granted as it used to be. In that sense, one now has to be far more professional.

I don't think monarchs should retire and be pensioned off, say, at sixty, as some professions and businesses stipulate. The nature of being a monarch is different.

Take Queen Victoria. In her eighties she was more loved, more known, more revered in her country than she'd ever been before.

In other walks of life too, age may bring accumulations of respect – and possibly wisdom – which are valuable to society. Looking at the monarchy as objectively as I can, I'd say retirement at a certain age is not a sensible idea. Some kind of unfitness is a different matter, but you must leave it to the monarch concerned.

If you look outside this country, King Gustav of Sweden reigned until he was ninety. I think most people agree that Sweden would have lost something had he retired at sixty.

There isn't any power. But there can be influence. The influence is in direct proportion to the respect people have for you.

ON THE BALCONY AT THE SILVER JUBILEE/ PHOTO CENTRAL PRESS

I'd change nothing. Besides ceremony being a major and important aspect of monarchy – something that has grown and developed over a thousand years in Britain – I happen to enjoy it enormously.

It's only right, I think, that in company with convicts, lunatics and peers of the realm, I'm ineligible to vote.

This is, of course, exactly as it should be: not necessarily in relation to convicts, but in relation to the monarchy.

The monarchy has done its best to adapt to changing circumstances, but

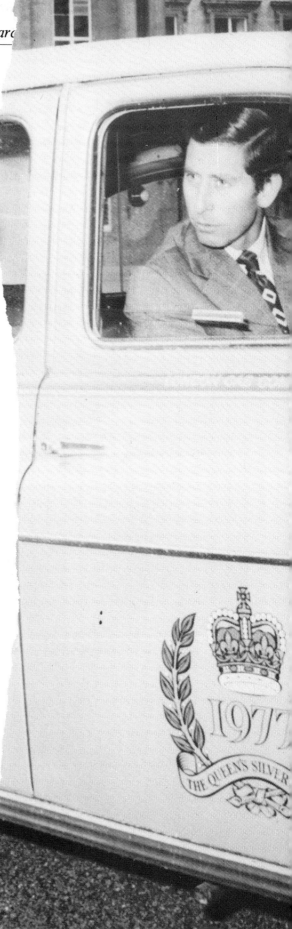

inevitably, it's more difficult to adapt when the accepted patterns of life and society are changing so unusually fast.

Monarchy is, I do believe, the system mankind has so far evolved which comes nearest to ensuring stable government.

I also believe that the institution of the monarchy – to which, rightly or wrongly, I belong and which I represent to the best of my ability – is one of the strongest factors in the continuance of stable government.

The Silver Jubilee.

It was great fun and, when done well and tastefully, there's nothing more marvellous than this sort of thing. Judging by the number of people in the streets, and their enthusiasm, they enjoyed it too.

AT THE HOUSE OF LORDS/BRITISH INFORMATION SERVICE

CHARLES IN A SILVER JUBILEE TAXI/PHOTO CENTRAL PRESS

Apart from anything else it was the most wonderful expression of happiness and affection for the Queen.

I felt it'd be marvellous if there was some permanent way in which we could mark the twenty-five years of service which the Queen has given to the country and the Commonwealth.

I asked my mother what she'd like us to do. After careful consideration, she said she'd be particularly pleased if money could be raised to assist and encourage the outstanding work already being done by young people in various fields.

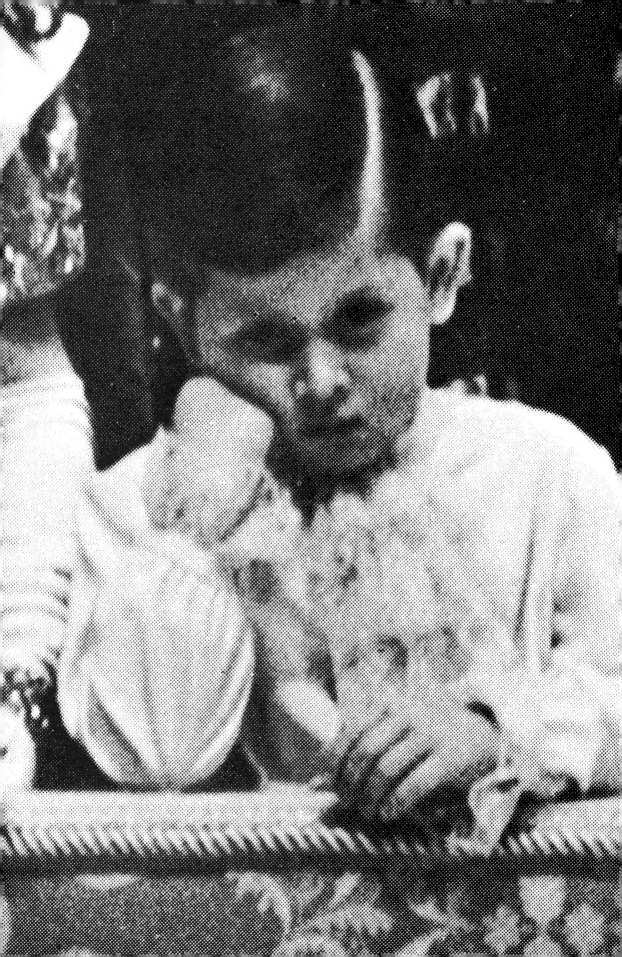

The Future King.

I think it's something that dawns on you with the most ghastly, inexorable sense. I didn't suddenly wake up in my pram one day and say, "Yippee," you know.

First, I thought of being the proverbial engine driver. Then I wanted to grow up to be a sailor, as I had been on the yacht for the first time, and, of course, a soldier, because I had been watching the Changing of the Guard. When I started shooting, I thought how marvellous it would be to be a big-game hunter. I went from one thing to the other until I realised I was rather stuck.

I think it dawns on you slowly, that people are interested in you ... and slowly you get the idea that you have a certain duty and responsibility. I think it's better that way, rather than someone suddenly telling you, "You must do this," or, "You must do that," because you are who you are. I think it's one of those things you grow up in.

I might not be king for forty years, so I don't know what my role will be.

My great problem is that I don't really know what my role in life is. At the

re King.

moment, I don't have one, but somehow I must find one for myself.

It's a fascinating job and I'm looking forward to the future.

I believe it best to confine myself to three basic aims at the start: to show concern for people, to display an interest in them as individuals, and to encourage them in a whole host of ways.

I've been trained to do it and I feel part of the job. I have this feeling of duty towards England, towards the United Kingdom

and towards the Commonwealth. I feel there's a great deal I can do if I'm given the chance to do it.

"I serve" is a marvellous motto to have, and I think that it's the basis of one's job.

If you have a sense of duty, and I like to think I have, then service is something that you give to people, particularly if they want you – but sometimes if they don't.

If you feel that you can do something…then you can be of service.

INSPECTING THE PARADE AT SANDHURST/PHOTO CENTRAL PRESS

This particular job is what I make it; you'll have to see what I do with it.

I think understanding on both sides is very important. I spend my life trying to understand others' problems. It's not easy, but I believe that it is most essential that one should have concern for people, help them get things off their chests.

I'm not much conscious of being a monarch-to-be. I'm much more conscious of being a Prince of Wales-as-is.

Yes, I suppose I *am* conscious of being different. You don't know – you can't know, can you? – how much different. After all, you only know what it is to be you, though you can study other people and deduce things about how *they* feel, to an extent.

But I've been brought up the way I have, and I've had the background I've had, and not many other people have had

that. So it does make one different, and make one feel different.

The most important thing for me is to have concern for people, to show it and provide some form of leadership.

I do worry about the future, but if one can preserve one's sense of humour, ability to adapt and, perhaps, help to calm things down and to provide a steadying influence, all will be well.

I think one has to be much more "with it" than of old, and much better informed.

I like to think I could be an ambassador not only for Wales, but also for the United Kingdom as a whole, and for one Commonwealth country to another.

I'm planning to find out all I can about British life, including the government, the civil service, agriculture, the unions and everything.

Britain & The British.

I've been all over the world and I always feel how marvellous it is to come back to Britain. You can read the papers when you're abroad and you think everything is coming to an end. But you discover that things are going on the same as always, and you feel happy to be back.

These things that are so important we take for granted . . . our traditions and our institutions. This long tradition of basic freedom, which, in so many cases, doesn't exist in other countries.

We need to be reminded of these very important essential freedoms, which, more than any others, make Britain what it is to us and what it is to other people. All over the world, people look to Britain for an example and a lead in so many different ways.

The country's morale can be seriously harmed by what the media choose, or don't choose to emphasise.

The British are past masters at self-denigration. Practised reasonably, that's an attractive trait. But sometimes we go too far and are only reminded of the few things that we don't do well, like the strikes that occur in a small proportion of our industries, or the unpleasant things that foreigners say about us rather than the infinitely more frequent complimentary remarks which they make.

I remember only too well, somebody telling me that, regrettably, it doesn't make news that fifty jumbo jets landed safely at Heathrow Airport yesterday; but it does make news if one doesn't. I still believe, however, in the necessity of reminding people – metaphorically – that vast numbers of jumbo jets do land safely.

Britain has indulged in far more self-depreciation than is good for her. There are millions of people who work incredibly hard and achieve magnificent things without any recognition whatsoever.

The British react so marvellously to hard times. I love this country and want to see Britain great again.

I think the distinguishing characteristic of British people is their ability to laugh at themselves, to anticipate events. The British are inclined to accept the inevitable and to adapt themselves to changing circumstances.

Industry.

Britain is a modern, up-to-date society which is still in the forefront of technological and industrial advance – from nuclear power to Concorde.

In the past few years, it would be true to say Britain has had an unfortunate image overseas, certainly as far as her industrial relations are concerned. We are constantly told that we are going to the dogs and are finished as a nation, by various American television commentators.

In actual fact, things are not nearly so bad as they are made out to be. In a survey conducted in industrial countries by the International Labour Office, it was shown that the number of days lost per thousand workers in Britain was lower than in the United States.

I am sure there are some parts of British industry which are good at dealing with innovation, but there are an awful lot of good ideas simply not being adopted.

There are two possible reasons for this: either a new idea seems too risky, or a

firm has its own ideas department which will jealously poo-poo anyone else's inspiration.

One of the great problems in Britain is to produce a marketable product from an invention. It seems people in Japan, France and America are much better at that than we are.

Charles speaks out:

I have not the slightest hesitation in making the observation that much of British manufacturing does not seem to understand the importance of the human factor.

I discovered during my recent visits that the problem of communication between management and the shop floor frequently stems from a failure of communications within management.

When front line managers are accused of poor communications, the truth is often that they cannot communicate because they don't know much themselves.

There is a sense in which the British managements remain inclined to play their cards very close to their chest in respect of company performance and plans.

This is not calculated to gain trust and co-operation from the work-force, which is essential if they are to co-operate with the introduction of change. People are not impossible to deal with.

Good British factories are very good, by any standards. The trouble is that there are not enough good ones. Why? Because the communication structure is inadequate.

A shop-stewards' convenor told of a manager who breezed in in the morning with a pipe firmly in the teeth, never bothered to acknowledge anyone and gave instructions to everyone. When he had a problem they all told him to get stuffed – probably through their shop floor supervisor.

British management might have something to learn from America. Their "single status" system, which is now beginning to be adopted by certain British companies, has a great deal to recommend it. Basically, it means that the

conditions of employment are the same whatever your position.

It also means eating in the same canteen.

Engineering:

Greater liaison and co-operation is necessary between industry and education in order to drag large parts of British manufacturing industry into the competitive 1980's.

British schools give high status to abstract learning and, as a result, practical experts like engineers have suffered a low status in Britain compared to overseas.

Engineers are too often seen as people who wear overalls, wield spanners and do dirty, undignified jobs.

What is badly needed, is action rather than sweet words. The various engineering organisations should stop arguing about who should be entitled to initiate any changes.

What is at stake, I believe, is the future success and potential prosperity of this country. If this arguing continues, there will be a distinct danger of becoming hopelessly bogged down and the best chance we have had for a long time... will be irrevocably lost.

The reason for my interest and concern is based on a simple observation: if we are going to regenerate industry in this country, to compete anywhere near successfully with our major competitors, and to create sufficient wealth to pay for such expensive luxuries as universities and all the other facilities we take for granted in modern society, then we have no alternative but to improve the status of the engineer and encourage those whose skills are essential to the manufacturing potential of the United Kingdom.

Attitudes in schools are crucial and the new degree course in electronic and electrical engineering at Bath was a bold initiative.

But many other universities were slow in introducing more practical and relevant subjects in response to the demand of a modern, technological society. There is definitely what can be described only as a "stick-in-the-mud" attitude in this sphere on the part of many universities.

I pray this will soon change to a positive realisation that adaptation to new and challenging circumstances *must* take place if we are to remain a major trading nation. Industry should not leave education to the academics and should make more practical training places available to graduates.

Engineers' skills are just as valuable as those of other professions, such as doctors and lawyers, but they have still not been recognised as such.

Our aim, therefore, should be to give potential engineers the chance they deserve and the moral encouragement they need so badly.

Reluctance and in-built conservatism would merely lead to a Pyrrhic victory for engineering. Nothing would be done and in the late twentieth century we'd merely find ourselves as one of the minor industrial states with no voice in international affairs, treated with pity, and, no doubt, with ridicule from time to time.

When asked to open a factory "very informally":
You mean you want me to drive a fork-lift truck through the wall?

On being addressed as "Charlie" by Yorkshire miners' leader, Joe Gormley:
I'm delighted to be called Charlie. It's better than the woman who jumped out of a crowd the other day and said, "Look, there's Action Man." It's better than in America, where they called you "prince." You do get fed up with being referred to like an RAF police dog.

Things are tending to change too quickly. People haven't had time to catch up

psychologically. This poses problems of all sorts: people don't really know where they stand; they don't know what's going to happen next and they can't plan for the future; they can't look ahead. Rapid change is something I find difficult to keep up with.

I believe strongly that one should adapt to changes, particularly in my position. You can't afford to get left miles behind.

Likewise, you don't want to be too far ahead. I think you always want to be just a little bit behind, but adapting gently and slowly, in some cases, taking the initiative and doing something before it's forced on you.

If you are taking it in the strictly economic sense, our competitors have managed to change much quicker than we have.

Mainly, it's because we were one of the few nations at the end of the last war that didn't actually lose out, so to speak. I come to the conclusion, looking around, that those who came off worst in the war had to change quickest.

It's an ugly fact to face sometimes, that economics, whether you like it or not, are here to stay. If you live in this particular world, you have to exist by trading and competing.

If you want, we can all drop out and live on little plots of land. Everybody may be much happier, but they're jolly well not going to have the things that we have now and that we take for granted – television, washing machines, cars and all these things. How the hell do they think we have all these, if it's not through our ability to produce the wealth to pay for them?

PHOTO METAL CONSTRUCTION

Young People.

I believe strongly that many more young people should be given the opportunity to find excitement and adventure through voluntary service and by organising themselves after initial help and training.

There are certainly plenty of things that young people could do, which involve an adventurous challenge and the responsibility of adulthood at a time when it's flattering and important to be considered as an adult.

The important thing is that the young people should run their own show. They don't want to do things which are planned and supervised by adults.

I often feel that in urban areas there's a distinct lack of facilities for younger people. I feel sometimes that the kind of attitude you see – particularly, for instance, at football matches – is really that they're trying to get rid of pent-up energy and enthusiasm. To my mind, it is misdirected.

I feel that they could be given opportunities – not just going to a football match, but other things – where they can get rid of their energy.

It's a problem that's always been with us, but more noticeably since the end of National Service.

Now, there's a limit as to how much of the adventure young people want can be combined with useful work.

But I'm sure you'll wave goodbye to any sense of adventure if you ask them to do only things that are suggested, laid on and directed by grown-ups. Especially by grown-ups who come from what they regard as "the Establishment" – the leaders of organisations which have been with us for many years – and are regarded, rightly or wrongly, by these young people as being hampered by class, religion or even a political outlook and background to which the young people don't subscribe.

It's not so much that they oppose these older people; they just feel they are remote, irrelevant.

PHOTO THE SUN

Youth: it's an awful word, really. Let's say "young people."

I'm now old enough, and I've seen enough, to worry about the alienation of young people from adult society. It's mainly in London and the big cities: I don't think it's so tough in the country.

What's wrong is that so many young people feel they don't belong, because they don't have a sense of service, of contributing. In the cities, the young coloured people feel this even more strongly.

The Queen's Silver Jubilee Appeal.

The central idea is this: there'd be a trust holding the funds.

Young people – including existing organisations – would come to the trust and say, "We want to do this. Will you give us the money?" The trust could then examine proposals; if they thought they'd work, they'd say, "Right, there's the money, and any help we can give. Get on with it."

Before we set up the trust – before it accepts the money which I believe is now available – we must be sure that the method will work and that enough young people will come forward to take advantage of it.

So, at the moment, there are pilot schemes being planned – one in Wales, one in Cornwall, one in London.

If they succeed, you'll hear more about the idea soon – and the trust will come into being, and work along those general lines.

Finance has to be supplied. There's got to be a certain amount of initial adult activity if the young people's projects are going to be launched. But as soon as they have got their own thing going, leave them alone.

I feel there's an alternative to bashing each other up at football matches, or whatever it is. It's just a question of getting them involved in more exciting things.

I happen to feel that you can involve more of the difficult type of person who one doesn't normally get to through the

PHOTO CENTRAL PRESS

medium of existing youth organisations. A lot of them are looking for kicks in some way or another and the kicks can be directed in a useful way.

There are lots of things chaps with motorcycles can do.

Let's help young blacks. Let's help the young help the old. All that goes without saying, but do you think there's anything we can do to help in Northern Ireland?

Immigration.

With supreme disregard for the dictates of caution and diplomacy, I urged that a great deal of good could be achieved by well-made films, primarily to explain to people living in this country the reasons for our behaviour, and to show the similarities that exist – even in the apparent differences between ourselves and other races.

My belief rested on the feeling that, if only more people could have the advantages of information and knowledge about other people's social behaviour, customs, religion and so forth, then perhaps some of the prejudice against immigrant groups in this country might be slowly reduced.

The more people understood about the background of our immigrants, the less apprehensive they would be about them. To get on neighbourly terms with people of other races and countries, you've got to get more familiar with them – know how they live, how they eat, how they work, what makes them laugh, their history.

I'm particularly fortunate in having seen different people in their own environments – many of which I have admired and found fascinating. It's easier, therefore, for me not to be prejudiced.

But it's difficult not to be prejudiced if they come and live in your street, and possibly the value of your property falls because of the new people arriving, and if you believe all the bad things you're told about them, because you don't know any better.

You can't remove people's apprehensions in one night, but you can make a start by making them more knowledge-able. If the Anthropological Society can help us to do that, I'm going to help it.

We hope to stimulate interest and knowledge and tolerance through new TV programmes – this is a field in which TV can be of immense assistance. Given that, as I say, you can't change attitudes or facts overnight, or in a year, you *can* speed up the rate at which people's minds change.

If you want examples of what I'd like to do in general, one thing is helping people and organisations to give us all more information about the problems we face as individual citizens.

Whatever cause I associate with, I want to *participate*.

Some organisations would be quite happy to have me as, say, patron, and just put my name on the literature. But I want to *do* something for it, with it, and through it.

I don't want to be a figure-head. I want to help get things done.

Wales.

In Wales, there isn't so much of a middle class as there is in England. The extra-ordinary thing about Welshmen is that they have this radical tradition – they are radically traditional and traditionally radical, and this is a curious paradox. They have an old tradition of support for the Labour Party, for instance, and yet, in the country regions, they are also very traditional in the more general sense of the word.

There's a certain amount of truth in saying that Wales has been neglected by a central government – it's on the fringes, and this has led to a certain depressed feeling and perhaps a slight inferiority complex, I'm not sure. At the same time, in Wales, as a result of their union with England, the upper strata of society moved off to England, and as it were relinquished their responsibilities towards the ordinary people.

As a result, the people of Wales have established their own folk culture, their own music, eisteddfods and folk dancing. Everything like that is unique to Wales, an essential part of the Welsh character.

England hasn't got anything like it.

Somebody was asking me the other day how England would like it if a Welshman was made Prince of England. Well, I don't think, in fact, English people would worry as much as the Welsh. It's not the same.

When I went to Llanelli not long ago, the mayor said, "Can you say 'Llanelli'?" I said; "Llanelli?," and he wiped the saliva out of his eye and said, "Well done."

I want to see as many people as possible in Wales show that they love their country as much as they say and sing they do.

The Commonwealth.

I don't think it would be a disaster if Britain withdrew from the Common-wealth; I'm sure it could survive without Britain. But I believe that the Queen, as head of the Commonwealth, plays an important part in keeping the whole thing together.

It's a wider family than it was and it is the Commonwealth and not the British Commonwealth. Too often, people are inclined to treat the concept of the Commonwealth with cynicism, or to reject it altogether as an anachronism and complete waste of everybody's time and effort.

Above all, I believe it is up to the young people of the Commonwealth to show that they believe that association has something to offer the modern world, because without their support, interest and encouragement, it will only be a matter of time before the whole thing fades away through lack of interest.

The whole question fascinates me. There's an enormous amount to be done there; the Commonwealth is one of those associations which require a great deal of effort and expertise to make it work satisfactorily and usefully in world terms.

I think there must be something unique about it, in that it has remained in being as long as it has. There must be some deep bond that's worth developing.

There must be something to be said for the Commonwealth, after all.

Ecology.

The future of our planet depends on the interest and involvement of the young in projects which improve the environment. Any work to improve the environment in the next few years would meet serious economic difficulties. We'll be faced with hard decisions about priorities.

It's not an impossible thing to achieve as long as it's realised that the countryside will not just stay here, serene and beautiful, unless countless individuals are determined it should do so.

We can achieve nothing without the immensely useful co-operation of the public and of the people who use the country most.

The aim is to create awareness that efforts in conservation and pollution control are designed for the long-term good of this country. To go on virtually destroying what we live in, until the final horror really strikes us, and then try to do something is

WEST NORFOLK HUNT AT HARPLEY DAME/PHOTO CENTRAL PRESS

WITH DAVID ATTENBOROUGH AT LIMEGROVE STUDIOS/CENTRAL PRESS

surely an insult to human rational thinking.

Charles was very impressed with the Canadian north:

Our own particular civilisation, if you can call it that, loses a great deal in an attempt to control nature. We must always remember that we are basically animals – and not to destroy any more of nature than is absolutely necessary.

Hunting:

I deeply revel in nature. I really do enjoy animals as such. It's part of man's curious instinct over thousands of years to go hunting – perhaps there is something wrong with my breeding.

Because you kill animals doesn't mean that you don't appreciate them fully or want to conserve them.

I think that if people did not partake in country sports in this country, there

would not be many animals left. There would not be the countryside we have now. It would be a basically average desert because most farmers would plough up hedges for more productive land.

It's because so many people enjoy hunting and shooting that the country remains as it is.

Cars:

Society committed to a machine that requires tracks to be scoured across the increasingly precious countryside, can either shrug its shoulders and excuse unoriginal and unimaginative road-building, or press for designs which harmonise, as far as possible, with the natural features of the countryside.

The Press.

Haven't you got enough pictures now?

However much one might inveigh against the Press – personally and collectively – I came to the conclusion long ago that there is always a price to be paid for freedom. A free Press is as much a part and a guarantor of our civilisation and liberty as any other factor.

There is, therefore, no question about the importance of a free Press in the world of the mid-Seventies. The right to report and criticise freely was hard won.

Charles composed this Ode to the Press while in Canada:

Impossible, unapproachable, God only knows,
The light's always dreadful and he won't damn-well pose,
Most maddening, most curious, he simply can't fail,

It's always the same with the old Prince of Wales.

Insistent, persistent, the Press never end,
One day they will drive me right round the bend,
Recording, rephrasing, every word that I say,
It's got to be news at the end of the day.

Disgraceful, most dangerous to share the same plane,
Denies me the chance to scratch and complain,
Oh where, may I ask, is the Monarchy going,
When Princes and pressmen are on the same Boeing?

The programme's so formal and highly arranged,
But haven't you heard that it's all been changed,

Friday is Sunday and that is quite plain,
So no one, please no one, is allowed
    to complain.

Honesty and integrity are vital factors (in reporting) and often get submerged in the general rush for sensationalism. The media has a large responsibility for the news it presents. The important thing is for truth to be actually portrayed.

The less people know about what is really going on, the easier it is to wield power and authority.

While many journalists approach their job with a strong sense of responsibility, the temptations to indulge in cynicism, sarcasm or sensationalism must be enormous. People believe what they read

in the papers. Even I find myself soaking up what the pages of print tell me.

I have read so many reports recently telling everyone who I am about to marry, that when last year a certain young lady was staying at Sandringham, a crowd of about ten thousand appeared when we went to church.

    Such was the obvious conviction that what they read was true I almost felt I had better espouse myself at once so as not to disappoint too many people. As you can see, I thought better of it.

From my sister's point of view, the behaviour of the photographers is very hard to take, and I can understand why. If you're doing something competitive in public, especially in the top international class, you are inevitably keyed up. To have a lot of people with cameras pursuing you,

and possibly frightening the horse, is annoying, to say the least.

It is easy to become irritable and to feel that it is only when things go wrong – when you are upside down or halfway up a tree – that photographs appear in the paper or on TV.

When I was younger, I sometimes used to get cross. Then, as I got older, I tried to think it out. I knew I mustn't go on being cross or shouting at people – it wasn't becoming in one so young.

So I tried to understand the other person's position and put myself in his shoes. Part of that means recognising the demands a newspaper makes of all the people who work on it, even if they own it.

Anyway, it's when nobody wants to write about you or take a photograph of you that you ought to worry in my sort of job.

Then there would be no point in being around – and I couldn't stand being around if there didn't seem to be any point to it.

Those foreign papers will report anything. One of them said I was having an affair with someone or other, the other day.

They are incredibly disreputable, but everybody reads them. They know it's nonsense but they love reading them.

Sometimes, particularly trivial stories about me appear. I suppose I must accept that what happens to me can be newsworthy, regardless of the context.